PRENTICE HALL

WORLD STUDIES
ASIA and the PACIFIC

Reading and Vocabulary Study Guide

PEARSON
Prentice Hall

Needham, Massachusetts
Upper Saddle River, New Jersey

The map on page 20 is based on a map by **DK Cartography.**

PEARSON
Prentice Hall

ISBN 0-13-128004-X

9 10 11 12 13 V011 14 13 12 11 10

Table of Contents

How to Use This Book 3

Chapter 1 East Asia: Physical Geography

Section 1 Land and Water 6
Section 2 Climate and Vegetation 9
Section 3 Natural Resources and Land Use 12
Chapter 1 Assessment 15

Chapter 2 South, Southwest, and Central Asia: Physical Geography

Section 1 South Asia: Physical Geography 16
Section 2 Southwest Asia: Physical Geography 19
Section 3 Central Asia: Physical Geography 22
Chapter 2 Assessment 25

Chapter 3 Southeast Asia and the Pacific Region: Physical Geography

Section 1 Southeast Asia: Physical Geography 26
Section 2 Australia and New Zealand: Physical Geography 29
Section 3 The Pacific Islands: Physical Geography 32
Chapter 3 Assessment 35

Chapter 4 East Asia: Cultures and History

Section 1 Historic Traditions 36
Section 2 People and Cultures 39
Chapter 4 Assessment 42

Chapter 5 South, Southwest, and Central Asia: Cultures and History

Section 1 South Asia: Cultures and History 43
Section 2 Southwest Asia: Cultures and History 46
Section 3 Central Asia: Cultures and History 49
Chapter 5 Assessment 52

Chapter 6 Southeast Asia and the Pacific Region: Cultures and History

Section 1	Southeast Asia: Cultures and History	53
Section 2	The Pacific Region: Cultures and History	56
Chapter 6	Assessment	59

Chapter 7 East Asia

Section 1	China: Transforming Itself	60
Section 2	Japan: Tradition and Change	63
Section 3	The Koreas: A Divided Land	66
Chapter 7	Assessment	69

Chapter 8 South, Southwest, and Central Asia

Section 1	India: In the Midst of Change	70
Section 2	Pakistan: An Economy Based on Agriculture	73
Section 3	Israel: Economics and Cultures	76
Section 4	Saudi Arabia: Oil and Islam	79
Section 5	The Stans: A Diverse Region	82
Chapter 8	Assessment	85

Chapter 9 Southeast Asia and the Pacific Region

Section 1	Vietnam: A Nation Rebuilds	86
Section 2	Australia: A Pacific Rim Country	89
Chapter 9	Assessment	92

How to Use This Book

The Reading and Vocabulary Study Guide was designed to help you understand World Studies content. It will also help you build your reading and vocabulary skills. Please take the time to look at the next few pages to see how it works!

The Prepare to Read page gets you ready to read each section.

Objectives from your textbook help you focus your reading.

With each chapter, you will study a Target Reading Skill. This skill is introduced in your textbook, but explained more here. Later, questions or activities in the margin will help you practice the skill.

You are given a new Vocabulary Strategy with each chapter. Questions or activities in the margin later will help you practice the strategy.

CHAPTER 1

Prepare to Read

Section 2 Climate and Vegetation

Objectives

1. Find out what kinds of climate Latin America has.
2. Learn what factors influence climate in Latin America.
3. Understand how climate and vegetation influence the ways people live.

Target Reading Skill

Preview and Predict Before you read, make a prediction or a guess about what you will be learning. Predicting is another way to set a purpose for reading. It will help you remember what you read. Follow these steps: (1) Preview the section title, objectives, headings, and table on the pages in Section 2. (2) Predict something you might learn about Latin America. Based on your preview, you will probably predict that you will learn more about Latin America's climate and plants.

List two facts that you predict you will learn about Latin America's climate and plants.

____

____

As you read, check your predictions. How correct were they? If they were not very accurate, try to pay closer attention when you preview.

Vocabulary Strategy

Using Context Clues to Determine Meaning You will probably come across words you haven't seen before when you read. Sometimes you can pick up clues about the meaning of an unfamiliar word by reading the words, phrases, and sentences that surround it. The underlined words in the sentences below give clues to the meaning of the word *dense*.

The Amazon rain forest is ***dense*** with plants and trees. The plant life is so crowded that almost no sunlight reaches the ground.

Unfamiliar Word	Clues	Meaning
dense	so crowded no sunlight	thick, close together crowded

Section Summary pages provide an easy-to-read summary of each section.

Provides a summary of the section's most important ideas.

Large blue headings correspond to large red headings in your textbook.

This checkmark tells you when to answer the Reading Check question.

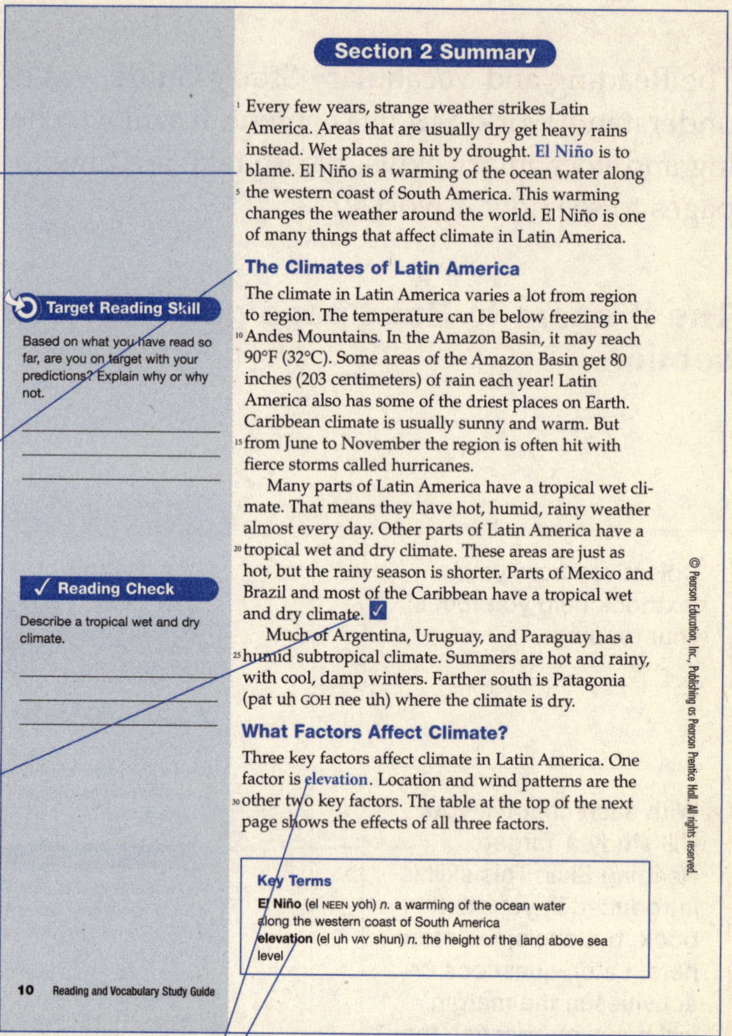

Section 2 Summary

Every few years, strange weather strikes Latin America. Areas that are usually dry get heavy rains instead. Wet places are hit by drought. **El Niño** is to blame. El Niño is a warming of the ocean water along the western coast of South America. This warming changes the weather around the world. El Niño is one of many things that affect climate in Latin America.

The Climates of Latin America

The climate in Latin America varies a lot from region to region. The temperature can be below freezing in the Andes Mountains. In the Amazon Basin, it may reach 90°F (32°C). Some areas of the Amazon Basin get 80 inches (203 centimeters) of rain each year! Latin America also has some of the driest places on Earth. Caribbean climate is usually sunny and warm. But from June to November the region is often hit with fierce storms called hurricanes.

Many parts of Latin America have a tropical wet climate. That means they have hot, humid, rainy weather almost every day. Other parts of Latin America have a tropical wet and dry climate. These areas are just as hot, but the rainy season is shorter. Parts of Mexico and Brazil and most of the Caribbean have a tropical wet and dry climate. ✓

Much of Argentina, Uruguay, and Paraguay has a humid subtropical climate. Summers are hot and rainy, with cool, damp winters. Farther south is Patagonia (pat uh GOH nee uh) where the climate is dry.

What Factors Affect Climate?

Three key factors affect climate in Latin America. One factor is **elevation**. Location and wind patterns are the other two key factors. The table at the top of the next page shows the effects of all three factors.

Target Reading Skill

Based on what you have read so far, are you on target with your predictions? Explain why or why not.

✓ Reading Check

Describe a tropical wet and dry climate.

Key Terms

El Niño (el NEEN yoh) *n.* a warming of the ocean water along the western coast of South America
elevation (el uh VAY shun) *n.* the height of the land above sea level

10 Reading and Vocabulary Study Guide

Key Terms, in blue within the summary, are defined at the bottom of the page.

Questions and activities in the margin help you take notes on main ideas, and practice the Target Reading Skill and Vocabulary Strategy.

Causes	Effects
Elevation	The higher the elevation, the colder the temperature
Location	Regions close to the Equator are warmer than those farther away ☑
Wind patterns	Sea breezes keep temperatures mild and bring more rain

Climate, Plants, and People

The Amazon rain forest is dense with thousands of types of plants. The air is hot and moist. In contrast, the Atacama (ah tah KAH mah) Desert in Chile has few signs of life because it is very dry. Latin America's physical features make such climate extremes possible.

Many regions of Latin America have less extreme climates. They have different kinds of vegetation, or plant life. Temperature and rainfall affect what plants grow in a region. They also affect what crops people can grow. For example, sugar cane, coffee, and bananas need warm weather and much rain. These three crops are important in Latin America. The **economy** of many countries depends on exporting these crops.

Elevation also affects vegetation. The higher the elevation, the cooler and drier it is. Plants must be able to survive in these conditions. ☑

Review Questions

1. What are four climates common in Latin America?

2. How does climate affect the people and the economy of Latin America?

Key Term

economy (ih KAHN uh mee) *n.* the ways that goods and services are made and brought to people

✓ Reading Check

How does being near to the Equator affect climate?

Vocabulary Strategy

Look at the word *vegetation* in the underlined sentence. Underline the surrounding words or phrases that are clues to the word's meaning.

Mark the Text

✓ Reading Check

Describe how elevation affects the vegetation of a region.

Chapter 1 Section 2 **11**

Use write-on lines to answer the questions. You can also use the lines to take notes.

When you see this symbol, mark the text as indicated.

Chapter 1 Assessment

...ree geographic regions of Latin America are
...exico, Brazil, and Peru.
...e Amazon, the Andes, and the Río de la Plata system.
...iddle America, the Caribbean, and South America.
...ral, isthmus, and tributary.

...mazon River is
...exico's greatest resource.
...e cause of hurricanes in the Caribbean each year.
...xt to the Andes Mountains in Chile.
...e of the largest rivers in the world.

...id subtropical climate is
A. one in which the weather is hot and rainy all year round.
B. hot, but the rainy season lasts only part of the year.
C. similar to the climate in parts of the southern United States.
D. found in the area called Patagonia.

4. Climate in Latin America is influenced by nearness to the Equator,
A. vegetation, and the economy.
B. elevation, and wind patterns.
C. location, and wind speed.
D. rivers, and deserts.

5. The amount of natural resources in Latin America can best be described as
A. the same throughout the region.
B. similar to that of the United States.
C. a sign of the region's economic diversity.
D. uneven from country to country.

Short Answer Question

How does the physical geography of Latin America affect the people who live there?

Chapter 1 Assessment **15**

Questions at the end of each section and chapter help you review content and assess your own understanding.

CHAPTER 1

Prepare to Read

Section 1 Land and Water

Objectives

1. Learn about the landforms and water bodies found in East Asia.
2. Find out where most of the people in East Asia live.

Target Reading Skill

Set a Purpose for Reading Reading a textbook is different from reading a novel or the newspaper. To read to learn effectively, you must preview and set a purpose for your reading.

Before you read this section, take a moment to preview it. Look at the title "Land and Water" and the objectives. Now flip through the next two pages. Read each heading. Headings tell you about the section's contents. They tell you what to expect to learn in the section. As you preview, use this information to give yourself a reason to read the section.

Are you curious about anything in the section, such as what a country with more than a billion people is like? Read to satisfy that curiosity—that's your purpose for reading.

Vocabulary Strategy

Recognizing Compound Words When you come across a new word, you may be able to figure out what it means if you break it down into parts. For example, if you do not know what the word *landform* means, you can break it down into its parts: *land* and *form*. A landform is a form, shape, or structure made from the land. Many words in English are made by combining two or more words. These words are called *compound words*.

Here are some common compound words that are made up of two words:

anybody	earthquake	farmland
highland	homeland	mainland
countryside	mountaintop	northeast

Section 1 Summary

Landforms and Water Bodies

One nation takes up most of East Asia's land. It is China. Mountains, highlands, and **plateaus** make up much of China's landscape. The other countries of East Asia also have mountains. But only China and Mongolia have wide plains and plateaus. The other countries—Japan, Taiwan, North Korea, and South Korea—have narrow plains. These plains lie mainly along coasts and rivers.

About 50 million years ago, the movement of the continents caused the land surface of Asia to fold and bend upwards. This process created the Himalayas and the Plateau of Tibet. The Himalayas are the highest mountain range in the world. They include Mount Everest, the highest mountain in the world. The Himalayas run along the border of China and Nepal. North of these mountains lies the Plateau of Tibet, a huge highland area.

Natural forces also shaped the islands of Japan. Earthquakes forced some parts of the country to rise and others to sink. Lava and ash from volcanos formed new mountains. Japan's Mount Fuji is a volcano, but it has not erupted since 1707. Volcanoes and earthquakes still change the shape of the land in parts of East Asia.

More people live in China than in any other country. How many? Over one billion people live there!

Two thirds of China's land is mountains and deserts. A desert is a dry place with few plants. The Gobi is a desert in China. It lies farther north than any other desert on Earth.

China's most important rivers are the Chang and the Huang. They begin in Tibet and flow east. The Chang River is deep enough for cargo ships. The Huang River runs through the North China Plain. The plain is very **fertile**. More than 100 million people live in this fertile area.

Key Terms

plateau (pla TOH) *n.* a raised area of level land bordered on one or more sides by steep slopes or cliffs

fertile (FUR tul) *adj.* able to support plant growth

Vocabulary Strategy

Mark the Text

The compound words below appear in this section. Draw a vertical line to separate the two words that form each compound word. Then circle the compound words in the text as you read them. Define each word.

highlands ______________________

____

earthquakes ______________________

____

Target Reading Skill

If your purpose was to learn about what China is like, list one fact from the bracketed paragraph that helps you meet your purpose.

Purpose: Learn about China.

Fact: ______________________

____

Japan is an **archipelago** in the western Pacific Ocean. It has four main islands. Most of Japan's people live along the coast. Nearly 80 percent of the country has mountains. ☑

The largest of Japan's islands is Honshu (hahn shoo). It also has the most people. Most of Japan's major cities are located there. Japan's capital city, Tokyo, is on Honshu.

Korea is a peninsula. That means it is surrounded on three sides by ocean. Korea is located between China and Japan. Since 1945, Korea has been divided into two countries. They are North Korea and South Korea.

✓ Reading Check

Is Japan a country of mountains or flat plains?

____

____

Population in East Asia

East Asia has almost 1.5 billion people. They are spread unevenly across the land. Few people live in the deserts, plateaus, and mountains. Most live on the plains and near the coasts because it is easier to grow food in those areas.

Places where many people live have a very high **population density**. The North China Plain is one example. It has a very high population density because it is level and has fertile soil. ☑

In East Asia, cities, farms, and industries are crowded onto the level land. Almost half the people of Japan live on less than 3 percent of the land. In China, most of the people live in the eastern half of the country. That is where the plains and coastal areas are.

✓ Reading Check

Why does the North China Plain have such a high population density?

____

____

____

Review Questions

1. What are the major landforms of East Asia?

____

____

2. In what areas do most people in East Asia live? Why?

____

____

Key Terms

archipelago (ahr kuh PEL uh goh) *n.* a group of islands

population density (pahp yuh LAY shun DEN suh tee) *n.* the average number of people living in a square mile or square kilometer

CHAPTER 1

Prepare to Read

Section 2 Climate and Vegetation

Objectives

1. Examine the major climate regions in East Asia.
2. Discover how climate affects people and vegetation in East Asia.

Target Reading Skill

Predict Making predictions about what you will learn from your text helps you set a purpose for reading. It also helps you remember what you have read. Before you begin reading, preview the section. Look at the section title and objectives above. Then look at the headings. Then based on your preview, predict what the section will tell you.

What do you think this section will tell you about the climate and vegetation of East Asia? List two facts that you expect to learn.

Prediction 1: ______________________________

Prediction 2: ______________________________

As you read, check your predictions. Were they right? If they were not very accurate, you may need to pay closer attention when you preview the section.

Vocabulary Strategy

Recognizing Roots Often, a few letters are added to the beginning or end of a word to make another word. For example, the letters *re-* may be attached to the beginning of a word. Or the letters *-ing* may be attached to the end of a word. When you add letters to a word, that word is called a root. A root is a word used to make other words. The word *play* is the root of the word *replay*. The word *carry* is the root of the word *carrying*. Adding letters to the root changes its meaning.

When you come across a new word, look at it closely. See if it contains a root word that you already know. If it does, then you're not far from understanding the word's meaning.

Section 2 Summary

East Asia's Climate Regions

There are five major climate regions in East Asia. They are semiarid, arid, humid subtropical, humid continental, and highland.

Much of eastern China has a **humid subtropical climate**. This means that the winters are cool, the summers are hot, and there is plenty of rain. The northeast is a **humid continental** area. There, summers are warm and winters are cold. In South Korea and Japan, summers are a bit cooler and winters a bit warmer than in other places at the same latitude. This is because these two countries are almost entirely surrounded by water.

The northern part of China is very dry. It has **arid** and **semiarid** climate regions. Temperatures there can be very hot or very cold. To the south, the Plateau of Tibet has a **highland** climate. It is cool and dry.

Monsoons are important to East Asia's climates. In summer, winds from the Pacific Ocean blow northwest toward Asia. They bring rainfall. It starts in June as a drizzle. In July, the rain gets heavier, and the winds cause hot, humid weather.

In winter, the winds change direction. They come from the northern part of Asia. They are icy cold and very dry. In parts of China, the winds cause dust storms that last for days. After they blow across ocean waters, they bring rain or snow to inland areas.

East Asia has hurricanes that are called **typhoons**. Whirling typhoon winds blow at high speeds of 74 miles an hour or more. The winds and heavy rains they bring can cause major damage. For example, in 1922, a typhoon that struck China caused about 60,000 deaths. ✓

Key Terms

monsoon (mahn SOON) *n.* a wind that changes direction with the change of season

typhoon (ty FOON) *n.* a hurricane or tropical storm that develops over the Pacific Ocean, with winds that reach speeds greater than 74 miles per hour

Target Reading Skill

Based on what you have read so far, are your predictions on target? If not, change your predictions now.

New Predictions: ____________

____

____

✓ Reading Check

How are typhoons different from monsoons?

____

____

____

The Influences of Climate

Climate affects what plants grow in East Asia. It also affects what crops people can raise on farms.

Much of East Asia's plant life is strong. It can stand the changes in temperature and rainfall that come with the change of seasons. For example, bamboo grows quickly during the wet season in southern China and Japan. But it can also survive dry spells. Even in China's deserts, plants will spring up quickly if it rains. **Deciduous** trees change with the seasons. Their leaves turn gold, orange, and red in the fall and then drop off.

Climate also affects life in East Asia. The region around the Huang River in China is a good example. The Chinese word *Huang* means "yellow." The river is named for the brownish-yellow soil called loess that is blown by the desert winds. The river carries the loess and leaves it on the North China Plain. This huge plain is one of the best farming areas in China.

The Huang River also floods. Dams help control the waters. But during monsoons, the river still sometimes overflows.

Climate also affects the diet of East Asians. Rice grows best in warm weather, so people in southern China grow and eat rice. In the cooler north, wheat grows better. People in the north eat more things made from wheat, such as noodles. ✓

Review Questions

1. What are the five major climate regions in East Asia?

____

____

____

2. How do monsoons affect climates in East Asia?

____

____

____

Key Term

deciduous (dee SIJ oo us) *adj.* describing plants that drop their leaves in the fall

Vocabulary Strategy

Each of the underlined words in the paragraphs to the left contains another word that is a root. Circle the roots you find in these words. The root of the first word, *quickly*, is *quick*.

✓ Reading Check

How does climate affect the diet of East Asians?

____

____

____

CHAPTER 1

Prepare to Read

Section 3
Natural Resources and Land Use

Objectives

1. Learn about East Asia's major natural resources.
2. Find out how the people of East Asia use land to produce food.

Target Reading Skill

Ask Questions Looking for the answers to specific questions as you read can help you understand and remember important ideas. Before you read this section, preview the section title, objectives, and headings to see what the section is about. What do you think are the most important ideas in the section? How can you tell?

After you preview the section, write two questions that will help you understand or remember important ideas or facts in the section. You might turn the headings into questions, such as:

- What are East Asia's natural resources?
- What are the mineral resources of the two Koreas?

Vocabulary Strategy

Using Word Parts Sometimes when you come across a new word, you can figure out what it means if you break it into parts. For example, look closely at the word *aquaculture*. You can break it into *aqua* and *culture*.

Think of other words you know that begin with *aqua*. Perhaps you have gone to an aquatic center to swim. You may know that an aquarium is a tank filled with water and used to keep fish in. Both *aquatic* and *aquarium* are words that have something to do with water.

Next, think of other words you know that end with *culture*. You probably know that *agriculture* refers to growing crops and raising farm animals.

Now, put what you know about the parts together. *Aquaculture* means "growing things in water."

Section 3 Summary

Natural resources are things found in nature that are useful to people. They include fertile land, minerals, water, and forests.

East Asia's Natural Resources

East Asia has many natural resources. The ones used for energy include coal, oil, and water for hydroelectric power. Other resources are raw materials that are used to make manufactured goods. Water and fertile land are important resources for growing food.

Some East Asian countries have more natural resources than others. For example, North Korea, a **developing country**, has coal and iron. South Korea, a **developed country**, has manufacturing. But it lacks coal and iron.

Mineral Resources of East Asia

Country	Resources
North Korea	**Has:** coal, iron
South Korea	**Imports:** iron, oil, chemicals
Japan	**Imports:** coal, natural gas, oil, iron, tin, copper
China	**Has:** coal, copper, tin, iron, oil

Both Koreas would benefit if they shared resources. But they are unfriendly to each other and do not share. So South Korea imports the materials it needs to make the manufactured goods it sells to other nations. It is one of East Asia's richest economies.

Japan is also a modern industrial society. It produces many manufactured goods even though it has to import huge amounts of minerals. In contrast, China has many mineral resources. It has one of the largest coal supplies in the world. ✓

Key Terms

developing country (dih VEL up ing KUN tree) *n.* a country where industry is not strong and there is little modern technology
developed country (dih VEL upt KUN tree) *n.* a country with many industries and a well-developed economy

Target Reading Skill

Turn the underlined sentence into a question. Read the paragraph and then write an answer to your question.

Question: ____________________

____

Answer: ____________________

____

✓ Reading Check

Based on what you have read, is Japan a developed country or a developing country?

____

____

East Asia's rivers can be used to produce hydroelectricity. That is electricity made by using the power of flowing water. Hydroelectric power is important to industry. But building dams and power plants is expensive. China is building a dam across the Chang River to produce more hydroelectric power. The Three Gorges Dam will also control flooding.

East Asia's waters are an important source of food. During the 1980s and 1990s, overfishing and pollution caused fish supplies to drop. That made aquaculture more important. Aquaculture is the farming of fish, shellfish, and seaweed. China is the leading aquaculture producer in East Asia.

Vocabulary Strategy

If you do not know what the word *overfishing* means, try breaking it into parts. In this case, over means "too much," as in *overeating* or *overgrown*. *Fishing* means "catching fish." What do you think overfishing is?

Using the Land to Produce Food

To feed the large population, East Asians need to farm every bit of land. With so many mountains and plateaus, only a small percentage of the land is level farmland.

In China, Japan, and parts of Korea, farmers cut **terraces** into steep hillsides. That gives them space to grow crops. Where climate and soil allow it, farmers use **double-cropping**. In China, farmers often plant one type of crop between the rows of another crop. In some parts of southern China, they can grow three crops in a year. In southern Japan, rice seedlings are replanted in a larger field after wheat has been harvested from it. ✓

✓ Reading Check

How do both terrace farming and double-cropping increase food supplies?

Review Questions

1. Name three natural resources in East Asia that can be used to produce energy.

2. How are both land and water used to produce food?

Key Terms

terrace (TEHR us) *n.* a flat area in a hillside
double-cropping (DUB ul KRAHP ing) *v.* growing two or more crops on the same land, in the same season, and at the same time

Chapter 1 Assessment

1. Which country takes up most of East Asia's land?
   A. Japan
   B. Mongolia
   C. China
   D. South Korea

2. Most of the people in Japan live
   A. along the coast.
   B. in mountainous areas.
   C. on Japan's wide plains.
   D. on plateaus.

3. How does the Huang River affect the North China Plain?
   A. It brings rain and snow.
   B. Its dams produce hydroelectricity.
   C. It carries soil to the area.
   D. It is used for cargo ships.

4. In East Asia, monsoons do NOT bring
   A. winds over 74 miles per hour.
   B. dust storms in the winter.
   C. summer rains.
   D. rain and snow to inland regions.

5. The mineral resources of East Asia are
   A. spread evenly among the countries.
   B. not spread evenly among the countries.
   C. located only in Japan.
   D. shared by North and South Korea.

Short Answer Question

How do Japan and South Korea make up for their lack of mineral resources?

____

____

____

____

CHAPTER 2

Prepare to Read

Section 1
South Asia: Physical Geography

Objectives

1. Learn about the landforms of South Asia.
2. Discover the most important factor that affects climate in South Asia.
3. Examine how people use the land and resources of South Asia.

Target Reading Skill

Reread or Read Ahead Have you ever replayed a scene from a video or DVD so you could figure out what was going on? Rereading a passage is like doing that. Sometimes you may not understand a sentence or a paragraph the first time you read it. When this happens, go back and read it again. You may need to read it two or more times.

Reading ahead can also help you understand something you are not sure of in the text. If you don't understand a word or passage, keep reading. The word or idea may be explained later. For example, you may be unsure of what it means when the Himalayas are called a barrier. If you keep reading, you will find an example of the Himalayas blocking cold air from the north.

Vocabulary Strategy

Using Context Clues Words work together to explain meaning. The meaning of a word may depend on the words around it, or context. The context gives you clues to a word's meaning.

Try this example. Say that you do not know the meaning of the word *subcontinent* in the following sentence:

> The Indian subcontinent was once attached to the eastern coast of Africa.

You could ask yourself: "What information does the sentence give me about the word?" Answer: "I know that a continent is a very large landmass. The sentence says the subcontinent was attached to Africa. A subcontinent could be a landmass that is smaller than a continent." In fact, a subcontinent is a large landmass that is a major part of a continent.

Section 1 Summary

The Indian **subcontinent** was once attached to eastern Africa. Then, 200 million years ago, it broke away and slowly slid toward Asia. About 40 million years ago, it collided with Asia. Northern India and southern Asia crumpled where they met. This formed the Himalayas, which include the world's highest mountains.

Major Landforms of South Asia

South Asia is shaped like a triangle. The narrow tip extends into the ocean. The largest nation in South Asia is India. Pakistan (PAK ih stan) and Afghanistan (af GAN ih stan) are west of India. The Himalayas form India's northern border with Nepal (nu PAWL) and Bhutan (BOO tahn). To the east is Bangladesh (BAHNG luh DESH). The island nations of Sri Lanka (sree LAHNG kuh) and the Maldives (MAL dyvz) are off the southern tip of India.

The Himalayas form a barrier between South Asia and the rest of Asia. They stretch about 1,550 miles (2,500 kilometers) from east to west. Mount Everest, the world's tallest mountain, is in the Himalayas.

Two major rivers in South Asia start high in the Himalayas. They are the Ganges and the Indus. The Ganges flows across northern India. It empties into the Bay of Bengal. The Indus flows west into Pakistan. Many people live in the plains around both rivers.

Along the Indus and Ganges rivers are huge **alluvial** plains. The rivers carry water and minerals needed for farming. The rich fertile soil makes this area good for farming. Many people live and farm here. Remember that South Asia is shaped like a triangle? At the southern point and going up both sides are two mountain ranges. They are the Western Ghats (gawts) and the Eastern Ghats. Between these mountain ranges is the Deccan Plateau. *Deccan* means "south" in Sanskrit. That will help you remember where it is located. ✓

Key Terms

subcontinent (SUB kahn tih nunt) *n.* a large landmass that is a major part of a continent
alluvial (uh LOO vee ul) *adj.* made of soil deposited by rivers

Target Reading Skill

Read ahead through the bracketed paragraph to see why the Ganges and Indus rivers are important to the people of South Asia.List one fact you discovered by reading ahead.

____

____

✓ Reading Check

Where is the Deccan Plateau located?

____

____

The Climates of South Asia

Monsoons are important to South Asia's climate. The summer monsoons blow over the Arabian Sea and the Indian Ocean and pick up moisture. When the air passes over the hot land of western India, it rises and loses its moisture in the form of rain.

The rains cool the coastal lands somewhat. Then the next air mass travels farther inland before losing its moisture. In this way, the monsoon rains work their way inland until they reach the Himalayas.

During the winter, the monsoons blow from the chilly northeast. <u>They move dry, frigid air toward South Asia</u>. But the Himalayas block the cold air. This means the countries of South Asia enjoy dry, mild winters. ✓

Land Use in South Asia

About 70 percent of South Asians live in rural areas. Most of these people are crowded into fertile river valleys. They grow whatever crops they can. ✓

Some countries grow **cash crops**. These include tea, cotton, coffee, and sugar cane. They can bring in a great deal of money. But when prices fall or when crops fail, farmers may not earn enough money.

India has many mineral resources. Iron ore and coal are plentiful. But India has only a small amount of oil, so it uses hydroelectricity and nuclear power.

South Asia is one of the most densely populated regions in the world. Most of the people live where there is plenty of rainfall. This includes coastal areas, northeastern India, and the country of Bangladesh.

Review Questions

1. Which landform is a natural barrier between South Asia and the rest of Asia?

____

____

2. List some cash crops raised in South Asia.

____

____

Key Term

cash crop (kash krahp) *n.* a crop that is raised or gathered to be sold for money on the local or world market

Vocabulary Strategy

What does the word *frigid* mean in the underlined sentence? Circle the clues in the surrounding words, phrases, or sentences that help you learn what *frigid* means. Define *frigid*.

Mark the Text

____

✓ Reading Check

Describe one way the summer monsoons differ from the winter monsoons.

____

____

✓ Reading Check

In what type of areas do most South Asians live?

____

____

____

CHAPTER 2

Prepare to Read

Section 2
Southwest Asia: Physical Geography

Objectives

1. Learn about the major landforms of Southwest Asia.
2. Find out what the two most important resources in Southwest Asia are.
3. Examine how people use the land in Southwest Asia.

Target Reading Skill

Paraphrase Paraphrasing is putting what you read into your own words. It is another skill that can help you understand and remember what you read.

Look at the first two paragraphs under the heading "A Dry Region Bordered by Water." They could be paraphrased like this:

> Southwest Asia is mostly desert. The world's largest desert covered entirely in sand is in Southwest Asia. Because there is very little rain, water is very valuable.

As you read, paraphrase the first paragraph or two after each heading.

Vocabulary Strategy

Using Context to Determine Meaning If you don't understand a word, sometimes you can pick up clues to its meaning from the words, phrases, and sentences around it. The underlined words in the paragraph below give clues to the meaning of the word *oasis*.

> Travelers passing through the desert are happy when they find an oasis. Sometimes, the <u>water from an oasis</u> can support a community of people. It <u>can be pumped from under ground</u> to irrigate crops and water livestock.

An oasis is a place in a desert region where fresh water is available from under ground. Do you see how the context clues help make that clear?

A Dry Region Bordered by Water

Southwest Asia: Climate Regions

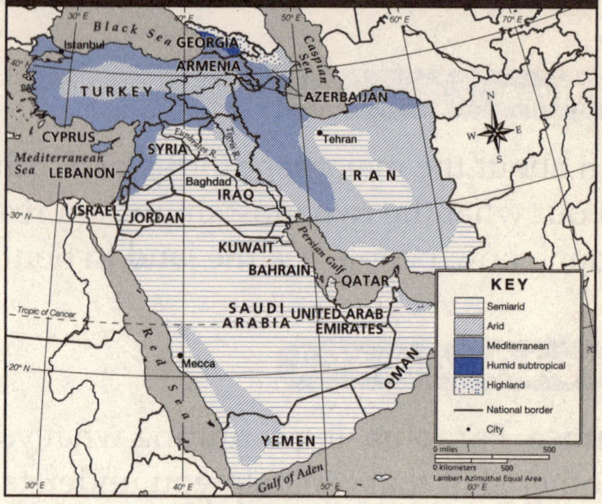

Most of Southwest Asia is desert. Less than 10 inches (25 centimeters) of rain fall a year. The Rub' al-Kahli is the world's largest all-sand desert. Ten years can go by between rainfalls. Not all deserts are covered with sand. Some include pebbles, gravel, and boulders.

Water is very valuable in Southwest Asia. Travelers in the desert are happy to find an **oasis**. An oasis in the desert can support a community. Farmers can grow crops. Nomadic shepherds can raise livestock.

There are some fertile areas in the region. The Tigris (TY gris) and Euphrates (yoo FRAYT eez) rivers begin in the mountains of Turkey and flow south through Iraq. When these rivers flood, they leave rich soil along their banks. In ancient times, one of the world's first civilizations grew up in this fertile area. The region was known as Mesopotamia. ✓

Southwest Asia is surrounded by water. Most of the region is hot and dry. But some parts of Southwest Asia have a Mediterranean climate. They have hot, dry summers but mild, rainy winters. The coasts of the Mediterranean, Black, and Caspian seas have a Mediterranean climate. So do the mountain areas.

✓ Reading Check

Where do the Tigris and Euphrates rivers begin?

____

____

Vocabulary Strategy

Look at the word *Mediterranean* in the underlined sentence. You may not have seen the word used this way before. But there are clues to what it means. Circle the words or phrases that help you learn its meaning in this context. Then write a definition of the term below.

Mark the Text

____

____

____

Key Term

oasis (oh AY sis) *n.* an area in a desert region where fresh water is usually available from an underground spring or well

Southwest Asia's Major Natural Resources

The two most important natural resources in Southwest Asia are **petroleum** and water. Petroleum, also called oil, is a **nonrenewable resource**.

We get gasoline and other fuels from petroleum. It is the natural resource that brings the most money into Southwest Asia. Since much of the region has a dry climate, water is the resource that people need most.

Southwest Asia is the largest oil-producing region in the world. Money from selling oil has improved the **standard of living** in many Southwest Asian countries. They have enough money to import goods and workers from other countries. The countries with little or no oil tend to have a lower standard of living. ☑

Most countries in the region must use irrigation to grow crops. People may use water from rivers or pump water from far underground.

Using the Land in Southwest Asia

Land in Southwest Asia is used for agriculture, nomadic herding, and producing oil. Most farmland is in the northern part of the region. The Mediterranean climate along the coasts lets people grow many crops.

For centuries, Bedouins (BED oo inz) have lived in Southwest Asia's deserts. They are Arabic-speaking nomadic herders. They move over a large area of land in search of grass and water for their animals. ☑

Review Questions

1. How do rivers and seas affect Southwest Asia?

____

____

2. Describe the different ways in which water and petroleum are important to Southwest Asia.

____

____

Key Terms

petroleum (puh TROH lee um) *n.* an oily liquid used as fuel
nonrenewable resource (nahn rih NOO uh bul REE sawrs) *n.* a natural resource that cannot be quickly replaced once it is used
standard of living (STAN durd uv LIV ing) *n.* a measurement of a person's or a group's education, housing, health, and nutrition

Target Reading Skill

Use your own words to paraphrase the bracketed paragraph. Be sure to explain what a nonrenewable resource is in your own terms. *Hint:* paraphrase the definition in the Key Terms box below.

____

____

✓ Reading Check

How has oil improved life in some countries of Southwest Asia?

____

____

____

✓ Reading Check

Who are the Bedouins?

____

____

____

CHAPTER 2

Prepare to Read

Section 3
Central Asia: Physical Geography

Objectives

1. Learn about the main physical features of Central Asia.
2. Discover which natural resources are important in Central Asia.
3. Find out how people use the land in Central Asia.

Target Reading Skill

Summarize When you summarize, you state the main points you have read. You leave out the less important details. A summary is shorter than the original text. When you summarize, keep the main ideas or facts in the correct order.

Look at the following sentence: "The Kara Kum desert covers much of the land in Turkmenistan, and the Kyzyl Kum desert covers much of neighboring Uzbekistan." It could be summarized like this: "Much of Turkmenistan and Uzbekistan is desert."

As you read about, pause to summarize the main ideas.

Vocabulary Strategy

Using Context to Clarify Meaning When you come across a word that you do not know, you can look for clues in the words and sentences just before and after the word. These clues are called context clues. They can include examples, explanations, or definitions. Also, you may already know something about the topic that gives you a clue. As you read, use the graphic organizer to help you.

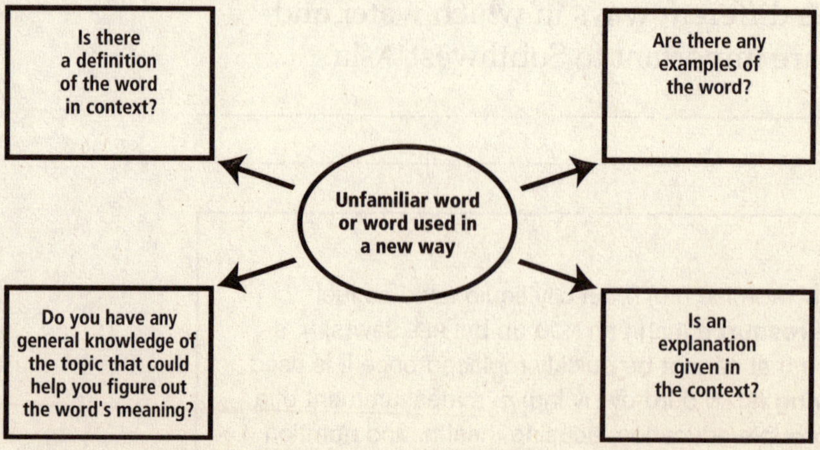

Section 3 Summary

Here are the countries of Central Asia. Kazakhstan (kah zahk STAHN) is the largest and northernmost country in Central Asia. To its south are Uzbekistan (ooz BEK ih stan), Kyrgyzstan (kihr gih STAN), Turkmenistan (turk MEN ih stan), and Tajikistan (tah jik ih STAN). Afghanistan forms the southern border of Central Asia. All of these countries except Afghanistan were once part of the Soviet Union.

Central Asia's Main Physical Features

Central Asia's main physical features are highlands, deserts, and **steppes**. The mountains are in the southeastern part of the region. The Tian Shan and the Pamir mountain ranges cover much of Kyrgyzstan and Tajikistan.

The land to the west of these mountain ranges is lower and flatter. The Kara Kum desert covers much of Turkmenistan. The Kyzyl Kum desert covers much of Uzbekistan. And the Kirghiz Steppe is located in nearby Kazakhstan.

Most of Central Asia has a dry climate. The interior is <u>arid</u>, or extremely dry. Around this dry region is a wide band of semiarid land, which gets a little more rain. ✓

There are two important bodies of water in this dry land. One is the Caspian Sea, which is really a salt lake. It is the largest lake in the world. It has some of the world's largest oil reserves.

The Aral Sea is located in the interior of Central Asia. It is also a salt lake. It was once the fourth-largest inland lake in the world. It has grown smaller since the 1960s because some of the lake has dried up. At that time, the former Soviet Union began using water from rivers that flow into the Aral to irrigate crops. This caused the lake to dry up.

Key Term

steppe (step) *n.* large, mostly level, treeless plains that are covered in grasses

Target Reading Skill

Summarize the bracketed paragraphs. Try to use 25 words or fewer.

✓ Reading Check

What type of climate does most of Central Asia have?

Vocabulary Strategy

Suppose you don't know what the underlined word *arid* means. Look at the context of the word for clues. Use the graphic organizer on the previous page to help you figure out what it means. Write a brief definition of *arid* below.

Natural Resources in Central Asia

Petroleum is a major natural resource in Central Asia. Another is natural gas. Kazakhstan, Uzbekistan, and Turkmenistan have large oil and gas reserves. Turkmenistan has the fifth-largest reserve of natural gas in the world. ☑

Central Asia has other valuable minerals as well. Kazakhstan has large deposits of coal. It exports much of its coal to former Soviet republics. The region also has major deposits of gold, copper, iron, lead, and uranium.

✓ Reading Check

What are two major natural resources in Central Asia?

1. ____________________

2. ____________________

Land Use in Central Asia

Most of the land in Central Asia is used for agriculture. Raising livestock and farming are both important. People in Central Asia have raised sheep, horses, goats, and camels for thousands of years. Cotton is a major crop.

Farming in Central Asia depends on irrigation. In the 1960s, the Soviet Union wanted to increase cotton production. Canals were built to carry water from two rivers to irrigate the cotton fields. Between 1960 and 1980, cotton production more than tripled.

This irrigation project took water from two rivers that flow into the Aral Sea. As a result, the Aral Sea began drying up. The land around the Aral Sea is also damaged. Huge amounts of pesticides were used on the cotton crops. These chemicals, which kill insects and weeds, have polluted the soil. The destruction of the Aral Sea is one of the world's worst environmental disasters. ☑

✓ Reading Check

How have pesticides damaged the land in Central Asia?

____

____

____

Review Questions

1. What are Central Asia's three main physical features?

____

____

____

2. What were the effects of irrigation on the Aral Sea?

____

____

____

Chapter 2 Assessment

1. The Indus and Ganges rivers make the plains of northern India good for
   A. mining.
   B. farming.
   C. aquaculture.
   D. hydroelectricity.

2. South Asian countries have climates with warm, dry winters because
   A. they are located along the Equator.
   B. they are located in a desert region.
   C. the Himalayas block cold air blown in by the winter monsoons.
   D. the Eastern Ghats block cold air blown in by the winter monsoons.

3. Most of Southwest Asia is
   A. irrigated by monsoons.
   B. covered by the Himalayas.
   C. covered by deserts.
   D. used for terrace farming.

4. Which brings the most money into Southwest Asia?
   A. water
   B. petroleum
   C. gold
   D. farm products

5. Farming in Central Asia depends on
   A. irrigation.
   B. monsoons.
   C. imported workers.
   D. traditional methods.

Short Answer Question

Why do you think one of the world's first civilizations grew up in Mesopotamia rather than elsewhere in Southwest Asia?

____

____

____

____

CHAPTER 3

Prepare to Read

Section 1
Southeast Asia: Physical Geography

Objectives

1. Learn about the major landforms of Southeast Asia.
2. Find out about the kinds of climate and vegetation in Southeast Asia.
3. Examine how people use the land and resources of Southeast Asia.

Target Reading Skill

Identify Main Ideas Have you ever asked someone, "What's your point?" With that question, you were asking for the main idea. Good readers look for the main ideas of what they read. To help you find the main idea of a paragraph, read it through once. Then ask yourself what the paragraph is about. Do all the sentences focus on the same subject? If so, you've found the main idea. Sometimes the main idea is stated directly in the first sentence or two.

The main idea of the paragraph below is underlined:

<u>Southeast Asia is divided into mainland and island areas.</u> The mainland is a peninsula. It juts out from the main part of Asia. The islands run east and west between the Indian and Pacific oceans.

Vocabulary Strategy

Using Context to Clarify Meaning When you come across new words in your text, they are often defined for you in context. Context is the nearby words and sentences. Sometimes the definition appears in a separate sentence. Sometimes there is a brief definition in the same sentence. Often, the word *or* is used to introduce the definition. Look at the following examples.

<u>subsistence farming</u>, or *farming that provides only enough food for a family*

<u>commercial farming</u>, or *raising crops and livestock for sale*

They grow rice in <u>paddies</u>. A <u>paddy</u> is a *level field that is flooded to grow rice.*

The underlined words are defined in context. In these examples, brief definitions appear in italics. When you come across a new word in your text, look both before and after the word for the definition of the word.

Section 1 Summary

The Land of Southeast Asia

Southeast Asia is divided into mainland and island areas. The mainland is a peninsula. It juts out from the main part of Asia. The islands run east and west between the Indian and Pacific oceans.

The nations on the mainland are Cambodia, Laos (LAH ohs), Malaysia (muh LAY zhuh), Myanmar (MYUN mahr), Thailand (TY land), and Vietnam. Malaysia is part of both mainland Southeast Asia and island Southeast Asia.

There are five major nations in island Southeast Asia. They are Singapore, Malaysia, Brunei (broo NY), Indonesia, and the Philippines. The largest of them is Indonesia. ✓

The islands are part of the Ring of Fire. It is a region of volcanoes and earthquakes that surrounds the Pacific Ocean. Some of the islands are the tops of underwater volcanoes.

Climate and Vegetation

Most of island Southeast Asia has a tropical wet climate with hot temperatures all year round. There is no dry season. Along the coast of mainland Southeast Asia, much of the land also has a tropical wet climate. But inland areas have a tropical wet and dry climate or a humid subtropical climate.

[Monsoons are important to Southeast Asia. There are two summer monsoons. One blows from the southwest, off the Indian Ocean. It hits the west coast. The other blows from the southeast, off the Pacific Ocean. It hits the southeast coast. Also, a winter monsoon blows from the northeast, off the Pacific Ocean. It hits the Philippines and Indonesia. (In the parts of Indonesia in the Southern Hemisphere, this is a summer monsoon.)]

The monsoons bring heavy rains that often cause flooding. All of this moisture supports tropical rain forests. The rain forests of Southeast Asia are green and thick with plants. ✓

Unfortunately, tropical climates also have typhoons. These are strong storms with high winds and heavy rain. They often cause property damage and loss of life.

✓ Reading Check

Name the largest nation in island Southeast Asia.

____

Target Reading Skill

Mark the Text

In the bracketed paragraph, underline the sentence that states the main idea.

✓ Reading Check

What are the results of Southeast Asia's monsoons?

____

____

____

Using the Land and Resources of Southeast Asia

Some people in Southeast Asia practice **subsistence farming**. They grow just enough food for their families. Others work on large plantations. This is one type of **commercial farming**. Cash crops grown there include coffee, tea, and rubber.

Rice has long been the main crop in Southeast Asia. It needs a hot climate and plenty of water. In fact, rice grows best when it is planted in water. In Southeast Asia, farmers use the **paddy** system to grow rice. Indonesia and Thailand are among the top rice producers in the world. Rice is also a main food for the local people.

Tropical rain forests cover large parts of the region. Many kinds of plants grow in them. They are a source of lumber, medicines, and chemicals. Unfortunately, huge areas have been cut down to provide lumber and create farmland. One result has been mudslides. Southeast Asia is trying to balance the need for economic growth with the need for rain forests. ☑

Bamboo is another forest resource. This grass has a woody stem and grows quickly. It is used to make houses, irrigation pipes, ropes, and bridges. Several Southeast Asian countries sell bamboo to other countries.

There are large amounts of oil and natural gas in the area. The countries of Southeast Asia use natural gas to make electricity. They do not need to buy oil from other countries.

✓ Reading Check

Why does Southeast Asia now have fewer areas of tropical rain forests than in the past?

___

___

___

Vocabulary Strategy

The term *bamboo* is defined in context. Circle its definition.

Mark the Text

Review Questions

1. Describe the climate of island Southeast Asia.

___

___

2. Why does rice grow well in Southeast Asia?

___

___

Key Terms

subsistence farming (sub SIS tuns FAHR ming) *n.* farming that provides only enough food for a family or for a village

commercial farming (kuh MUR shul FAHR ming) *n.* raising crops and livestock for sale on the local or world market

paddy (PAD ee) *n.* a level field that is flooded to grow rice

CHAPTER 3

Prepare to Read

Section 2
Australia and New Zealand: Physical Geography

Objectives

1. Find out why Australia and New Zealand have unique physical environments.
2. Learn about Australia's physical geography.
3. Explore New Zealand's physical geography.

Target Reading Skill

Identify Supporting Details The main idea of a paragraph or section is its most important point. The main idea is supported by details. Details give more information about the main idea. They tell you *what, where, why, how much*, or *how many*.

The main idea of the paragraphs under the heading "Unique Physical Environments" is given below.

Australia and New Zealand have plants and animals like nowhere else because they are located far from other continents.

When you read, notice how the details in these paragraphs tell you more about the features that are special to Australia and New Zealand, and how and why they happened.

Vocabulary Strategy

Using Context to Clarify Meaning When you come across a word that you do not know, you may not need to look it up in a dictionary. Continue to read to the end of the paragraph. See if you can figure out what the word means from its context, or the words and sentences near the unfamiliar word. Context clues can include examples and explanations. In this example, the context clues to one meaning of the underlined word are in italics.

<u>Marsupials</u> include *kangaroos, koalas*, and *opossum*.

How do the examples help you understand the word *marsupials*?

✓ Reading Check

In which hemisphere are Australia and New Zealand located?

Vocabulary Strategy

From context clues, write a definition of the word *unique*. Circle words or phrases in the text that helped you write your definition.

Mark the Text

Target Reading Skill

Which detail in the bracketed paragraph supports the main idea—that the plants and animals of Australia and New Zealand are not like those elsewhere?

✓ Reading Check

Why are Australia's east and southeast coasts good places to live?

Section 2 Summary

Unique Physical Environments

Australia and New Zealand lie between the Pacific and Indian oceans. They are both in the Southern Hemisphere (south of the Equator). So their seasons are the opposite of those in the United States. ✓

New Zealand and Australia are very far from other continents. Many of their plants and animals are unique. They are found nowhere else on Earth. For example, kiwi and yellow-eyed penguins live only in New Zealand. And kangaroos and koalas live only in Australia. These last two animals are **marsupials**. In Australia, almost all mammals are marsupials. This is not true anywhere else in the world.

The animals of Australia and New Zealand are unique, or one of a kind, because of their isolation. The movement of **tectonic plates**—parts of the Earth's crust—caused their isolation. Australia, New Zealand, and the Pacific islands are on a tectonic plate that was once part of Africa. Hundreds of millions of years ago, this plate broke away from Africa. It moved slowly—an inch or two a year—toward Asia.

Over the centuries, small changes have occurred naturally in the animals and plants of Australia and the islands. For example, many birds have lost the ability to fly. Because they are so far from other landmasses, these animals have not spread to other regions.

Australia's Physical Geography

Australia is Earth's smallest continent. It is about the size of the United States without Alaska and Hawaii.

Winds blowing across the Pacific Ocean bring rain and a mild and pleasant climate to the east coast. Most Australians live in cities along Australia's east and southeast coasts. Rivers flow through fertile farmland in the southeast part of the country. ✓

Key Terms

marsupial (mahr SOO pea ul) *n.* an animal, such as a kangaroo, that carries its young in a body pouch

tectonic plate (tek TAHN ik playt) *n.* a huge slab of rock that moves very slowly over a softer layer beneath the surface of Earth's crust

New Zealand's Physical Geography

New Zealand is much smaller than Australia. It is made up of two major islands, North Island and South Island. Both islands have forests, lakes, and mountains. The islands were formed by volcanoes.

New Zealand's climate is cooler than Australia's because it is farther from the Equator. Also, no place in New Zealand is very far from the ocean. As a result, the country has a mild climate and plenty of rainfall.

There is a volcanic plateau in the middle of North Island. It includes three active volcanoes. North of the volcanoes, **geysers** shoot hot water into the air. New Zealanders use this energy to produce electricity. New Zealand's capital, Wellington, is located on North Island. So is its largest city, Auckland.

South Island has a high mountain range called the Southern Alps. Glaciers cover the mountains. There are also lakes and **fiords**. To the southeast is the flat, fertile Canterbury Plain. Most of New Zealand's crops are grown here. Ranchers also raise sheep and cattle. ✓

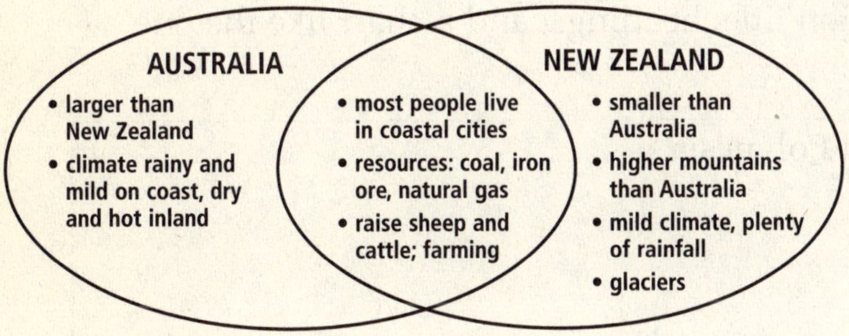

✓ Reading Check

Why is the Canterbury Plain important to New Zealand?

____

____

____

Review Questions

1. Describe the way that Australia and New Zealand became isolated from other continents.

____

____

2. How were the islands of New Zealand formed?

____

____

Key Terms

geyser (GY zur) *n.* a hot spring that shoots a jet of water and steam into the air

fiord (fyawrd) *n.* a long, narrow stretch of the sea bordered by steep slopes that were created by glaciers

CHAPTER 3

Prepare to Read

Section 3
The Pacific Islands: Physical Geography

Objectives

1. Examine features of high islands and low islands.
2. Learn about the three main island groups.
3. Find out what kind of climate and vegetation the islands have.
4. Discover how land is used in the Pacific islands.

Target Reading Skill

Identify Main Ideas How can you find the main idea of a section or paragraph if it is not stated directly? Sometimes as a reader you have to work a little harder to find out what the main idea is. Sometimes it is up to you to put all the details together and come up with the main idea.

Let's say you just finished reading the paragraphs under the heading "Melanesia, Micronesia, and Polynesia" and you noted that the main idea was not stated. Use the section title, headings, and a chart like the one below to find the main idea.

Melanesia, Micronesia, and Polynesia Details: 1. 2. 3.
Main Idea:

Vocabulary Strategy

Using Context to Clarify Meaning When you come across a word that you do not know, you may not need to look it up in the dictionary. In this workbook, key terms appear in blue. The definitions are in a box at the bottom of the page. Looking at the definition breaks up your reading. Before you do that, continue to read to the end of the paragraph. See if you can figure out what the word means from its context. Clues can include examples and explanations. Then look at the definition on the bottom of the page to see how accurate you were. Finally, reread the paragraph to make sure you understood what you read.

Section 3 Summary

The Pacific Ocean covers nearly one third of Earth's surface. It is dotted with thousands of islands. They include the second-largest island in the world, New Guinea. They also include the world's smallest island nation, Nauru (NAH oo roo). It is just 8 square miles (21 square kilometers).

The Pacific islands are divided into three main groups—Melanesia (mel uh NEE zhuh), Micronesia (my kruh NEE zhuh), and Polynesia (pahl uh NEE zhuh). Each of these groups covers a particular area.

High Islands and Low Islands

Pacific islands are also divided into high islands and low islands. **High islands** are mountainous. They have been formed by volcanoes. Their fertile soil is made up of volcanic ash. Because of their larger size and because people can grow crops there, high islands can support more people than low islands can. ✓

Low islands are made up of **coral** reefs or **atolls**. Far fewer people live there. This is partly because low islands are very small. Also, they have poor, sandy soil and little fresh water. It is hard to raise crops on them. Most people on low islands survive by fishing.

Melanesia, Micronesia, and Polynesia

The island group with the most people is Melanesia. It is north and east of Australia. Most of its large islands are high islands. New Guinea, Fiji, and the Solomon Islands are part of Melanesia.

Micronesia is mostly low islands. It covers an area of the Pacific the size of the continental United States. Most of the islands are north of the Equator and very small. The largest is Guam.

Key Terms

high island (hy EYE lund) *n.* an island formed from the mountainous top of an ancient volcano

low island (loh EYE lund) *n.* an island formed from coral reefs or atolls

coral (KAWR ul) *n.* a rocklike material made up of the skeletons of tiny sea creatures

atoll (A tawl) *n.* a small coral island in the shape of a ring

Target Reading Skill

In one sentence, state the main idea of the bracketed paragraphs.

____

____

____

Vocabulary Strategy

Before you read the definition *high island* in the box below, try to use context to understand the word. Circle any words or phrases that give you clues.

Mark the Text

✓ Reading Check

On which type of island do most Pacific island people live? Why?

____

____

____

✓ Reading Check

Which island group is Hawaii part of?

______

✓ Reading Check

Why do low islands have little vegetation?

______

✓ Reading Check

Give two examples of cash crops grown in the Pacific islands.

______

Polynesia is the largest island group in the Pacific. It includes the state of Hawaii. Polynesia has many high islands, including Tahiti and Samoa. Their high volcanic mountains are covered by dense rain forests. Along the shores are sandy beaches with palm trees. Tonga is one of Polynesia's few low islands. ☑

Climate and Vegetation of the Pacific Islands

The Pacific islands are in the tropics. Temperatures are hot all year. But ocean winds keep the temperatures from getting too high.

Some Pacific islands have wet and dry seasons. However, most of them get heavy rainfall all year long. Some low islands get only scattered rainfall.

The rich vegetation of the high islands is a result of their high temperatures, plentiful rainfall, and fertile soil. Hills are covered by tropical rain forests. Savanna grasses grow in the lowlands. However, low islands have little vegetation. Their poor soil supports only palm trees, grasses, and small shrubs. ☑

Natural Resources and Land Use

The Pacific island region has few natural resources. The most important one is the coconut palm. It provides food, clothing, and shelter. Another important resource is fish.

Some Pacific island countries grow cash crops. For example, Fiji produces sugar cane. Another important cash crop in the region is copra. It is dried coconut. It is used in margarine, cooking oils, soaps, and cosmetics. ☑

The Pacific islands' most valuable resource may be their natural beauty. Tourism is an important source of income in the region.

Review Questions

1. Name the three Pacific island groups.

______

2. Tell the difference between high islands and low islands in the Pacific.

______

Chapter 3 Assessment

1. Thailand, Cambodia, and Vietnam are part of
   A. island Southeast Asia.
   B. Polynesia.
   C. Micronesia.
   D. mainland Southeast Asia.

2. The region of volcanoes and earthquakes surrounding the Pacific Ocean is called
   A. coral atolls.
   B. high islands.
   C. Malaysia.
   D. the Ring of Fire.

3. Where do most Australians live?
   A. along the west and northern coasts
   B. along the east and southeast coasts
   C. along the west and southern coasts
   D. in the center of the country

4. New Zealanders use the energy from __________ to produce electricity.
   A. volcanoes
   B. coral
   C. earthquakes
   D. geysers

5. Pacific island natural resources include
   A. margarine, cooking oil, and soap.
   B. paddies, monsoons, and typhoons.
   C. coconut palm, fish, and their natural beauty.
   D. oil, natural gas, and water.

Short Answer Question

Why would a subsistence farmer in Southeast Asia raise rice instead of rubber?

____

____

____

____

CHAPTER 4

Prepare to Read

Section 1 Historic Traditions

Objectives

1. Learn about civilizations of East Asia.
2. Learn how Chinese culture influenced the rest of East Asia.
3. Find out how East Asia was affected by Western nations.

Target Reading Skill

Use Context Clues What can you do when you see a word used in an unfamiliar way? You could look the word up in a dictionary. But often you can get a good idea of what the word means from its context. A word's context is the words and sentences around it.

Let's use the word *emperor* as an example. The context may give clues about the word, as in the first example below. Or it may give the word's definition, as in the second example. Read the examples.

> Ancient China had an emperor. This man was the ruler of the empire, which is similar to being the president of a country.

> Ancient China was ruled by an emperor—a male ruler of an empire.

Did you figure out that an emperor is a male ruler of an empire?

Vocabulary Strategy

Recognizing Signal Words Have you ever noticed road signs that say "Rest Stop 10 Miles Ahead" or "Last Gas for Next 30 Miles"? Road signs prepare you for what is coming next. In the same way, when you read text, signal words prepare you for what is coming next.

Some signal words show time. They let you know the order in which events take place.

Some examples of signal words or phrases that show time are given in the box below.

then	when	around 1650
in 1808	later	earlier
as early as 200 B.C.	in time	

Section 1 Summary

Civilizations of East Asia

Important Parts of a Civilization	
cities	social classes
a central government, which rules the entire area	workers who are good at particular jobs

The Chinese civilization has existed longer than any other civilization. For centuries, China kept to itself. The proud leaders called China the Middle Kingdom. To them, China was the center of the universe.

The ancient Chinese invented paper, gunpowder, silk weaving, the magnetic compass, the printing press, and clockworks. They also built canals, dams, bridges, and irrigation systems. ☑

Starting in ancient times, China was governed by **emperors**. Since that time, China has been ruled by eight major **dynasties**.

Another civilization arose in Korea. Korea's history is closely tied to China's. For example, settlers from China shared Chinese knowledge and customs with the Koreans. Korea was also ruled by dynasties, but only three. The first one, called the Shilla dynasty, unified Korea as one country in A.D. 668.

An early civilization also developed in Japan. For much of Japan's history, **clans** fought each other for land and power. Around A.D. 500, the Yamato (yah MAH toh) clan became powerful. Their leaders made themselves emperors, but they had little power. For more than 700 years, shoguns (SHOH gunz), or "emperor's generals," made Japan's laws. Warriors called samurai (SAM uh ry) enforced the laws.

Japan did not deal with other countries from about 1640 to 1853. Its rulers believed that this would keep the country united.

Key Terms

emperor (EM pur ur) *n.* a male ruler of an empire
dynasty (DY nus tee) *n.* a number of rulers in a row who are from the same family
clan (klan) *n.* a group of families who share the same ancestor

✓ Reading Check

Name four inventions of the Chinese.

____
____
____
____

Target Reading Skill

Look for the underlined word *unified*. Circle the phrase in the sentence that provides a context clue for unified.

Mark the Text

Vocabulary Strategy

As you read this page, look for the following signal words and phrases that indicate when something happened. Circle the signal words when you find them.

later
in 1899
around the same time
after World War II

✓ Reading Check

Give an example of something that spread from China to Korea and Japan through cultural diffusion.

✓ Reading Check

How did Japan cause the start of World War II in East Asia?

The Spread of Cultures in East Asia

Many Chinese discoveries spread to Korea and Japan. This spreading of ideas is called **cultural diffusion**. Beliefs also spread. For example, the religion of Buddhism (BOOD iz um) had come to China from India. Later, it spread from China to Korea and Japan. ☑

Westerners in East Asia

During the 1800s, Europeans and Americans wanted to sell products in East Asia. In 1853, U.S. Commodore Matthew Perry sailed to Japan with four warships. He forced Japan to begin trading with the United States. In 1899, the United States announced that China, too, would be open for trade, and with all nations.

The Chinese blamed the emperor for the situation. In 1911, a revolution broke out in China. Instead of an empire, a republic was then set up.

Around the same time, Japan began wanting to control other Asian countries. Japan wanted their resources. In 1941, Japan caused the start of World War II in East Asia by attacking nearby countries. The United States and its allies defeated Japan in 1945. ☑

After World War II, civil war broke out in China between the Nationalists and the Communists. The Communists won in 1949. They turned China into a **communist** nation. Korea was split into two parts after World War II. In 1950, communist North Korea invaded South Korea. The United States sent troops to help South Korea. They fought for three years. But neither side won. Korea is still two countries today.

Review Questions

1. Who ruled East Asia's ancient civilization?

2. Why did Matthew Perry sail to Japan in 1853?

Key Terms

cultural diffusion (KUL chur ul dih FYOO zhun) *n.* the spreading of ideas or practices from one culture to other cultures
communist (KAHM yoo nist) *adj.* having a government that controls the country's large industries, businesses, and land

CHAPTER 4

Prepare to Read

Section 2 People and Cultures

Objectives

1. Examine some ways in which East Asia's past affects its modern-day culture.
2. Find out how the people of China are different from the people of the Koreas and Japan.

Target Reading Skill

Use Context Clues Sometimes as you read, you come across a word or phrase that does not make sense to you. Often when this happens, you can use context clues and your own general knowledge to figure out what the word means.

Sometimes you will find a context clue in the same sentence as the word or phrase you want to understand. Other times, you may need to keep reading to find a context clue. On the next page, you will find the sentence *Marriages are still arranged*. You may not understand what *arranged* means when used this way. But keep reading and you will find out:

> In an arranged marriage, parents or other family members decide who will marry whom.

Vocabulary Strategy

Recognizing Signal Words Signal words are words or phrases that give you clues or directions when reading. Some signal words or phrases explain how what you just read connects to what you will read next. These words or phrases help signal causes or effects of events that you are reading about.

Words/phrases that signal causes:	Words/phrases that signal effects:
because	as a result
if	so
since	then
on account of	therefore

Section 2 Summary

Target Reading Skill

Use the bracketed paragraph to help you define *private land ownership*. Circle the phrases that give you clues. Then write a definition below.

____

____

____

Tradition and Change

In 1949, the Communists took power in China. They began making changes to China's traditions. For example, people used to own their own farms and land. The government replaced the old system of private land ownership with **communes**.

Many farmers were used to working in family groups in small fields. They refused to work in the communes. So the communes did not produce enough food for all the people. Food production finally increased when the government allowed some private land ownership.

Another change began in the 1970s. China's population was large. The Communists tried to slow its growth by keeping families small. Couples were supposed to marry later and have only one child.

The Communists also changed women's rights. They passed a law allowing a woman to own property, choose her husband, and get a divorce. But today, men still hold most of the power. Marriages are still arranged. In an arranged marriage, parents or other family members decide who will marry whom.

In East Asia today, tradition and change mix in many ways. In China, old traditions are strongest in the countryside. But they do exist in the cities. Tiny shops sit next to modern buildings. People may ride in cars or in three-wheeled taxis that are pedaled like a bike.

In both Koreas, daily life is influenced by traditions. The family is important. But families today are smaller than before. In the countryside, grandparents, parents, aunts, and uncles may live in one household. In cities, usually only parents and children live together. The role of women has also changed. In the past, Korean women had few opportunities. Today, women can work and vote.

Japan is the most modern East Asian country. There, people use many modern technologies. Nearly 80 percent of Japan's people live in cities. At the same time,

Key Term

commune (KAHM yoon) *n.* a community in which people own land as a group and where they live and work together

many people still follow traditional customs at home. For example, at home they may wear kimonos, or robes, and sit on mats at a low table to eat. ☑

East Asia's People

East Asia is a mix of old and new cultures. Within each country, though, people tend to share a single culture.

About 19 of every 20 Chinese people are from the Han **ethnic group**. The Han live mostly in eastern China. All Han use the same written language. But they speak different **dialects** from one region to another.

The other Chinese come from 55 different minority groups. These groups live mainly in western and southern China. In terms of ethnic groups, China has more diversity than most other countries. ☑

Korea has much less diversity. Historians believe that the ancient Korean language was brought by **nomads** from the north. Over time, these groups came to share the same traditions. The population became **homogeneous**. That means the people are all very alike. There are few minority groups in the Koreas today.

[Japan is an island nation. And for many years, it did not deal with the rest of the world. For these reasons, it has one of the most homogeneous populations on Earth. Nearly all of Japan's people belong to the same ethnic group. Japan also makes it hard for anyone who is not Japanese to become a citizen.

Review Questions

1. What changes did the Communists make in China?

____

____

2. To which ethnic group do most Chinese belong?

____

____

Key Terms

ethnic group (ETH nik groop) *n.* a group of people who share such characteristics as language, religion, and ancestry
dialect (DY uh lekt) *n.* a variation of a language that is spoken in a particular region or area
nomad (NOH mad) *n.* a person who has no settled home but who moves from place to place
homogeneous (hoh moh JEE nee us) *adj.* identical or similar

✓ Reading Check

Which is the most modern country in East Asia?

____

____

____

✓ Reading Check

How is the population of China different from the populations of most other countries?

____

____

____

Vocabulary Strategy

In the bracketed paragraph, a signal word or phrase is used to show cause and effect. Find the signal word and circle it. Then write the cause and effect below.

Cause: ____________________

____

Effect: ____________________

____

Chapter 4 Assessment

1. Which civilization has existed longer than any other civilization?
   A. China
   B. North Korea
   C. South Korea
   D. Japan

2. Why did Japanese leaders want to avoid dealing with other countries?
   A. They did not want to buy goods from other lands.
   B. They did not have enough goods to sell to other countries.
   C. They believed that it would keep the country united.
   D. They did not want to learn foreign languages and customs.

3. Buddhism spread from China to the Koreas. This is an example of
   A. cultural migration.
   B. irrigation.
   C. cultural diffusion.
   D. Communist rule.

4. How did the rights of Chinese women change under communism?
   A. They lost many of their old rights.
   B. They were often forced to marry husbands they did not choose.
   C. They were no longer allowed to get a divorce.
   D. They were allowed to own property.

5. Which country in East Asia has the greatest number of ethnic groups?
   A. North Korea
   B. South Korea
   C. China
   D. Japan

Short Answer Question

What are the important parts of a civilization?

____

____

____

____

CHAPTER 5

Prepare to Read

Section 1
South Asia: Cultures and History

Objectives

1. Find out which religions became part of South Asian cultures.
2. Understand which empires shaped the history of South Asia.
3. Learn about the present-day religions and languages of South Asian cultures.

Target Reading Skill

Analyze Word Parts Often, when you come across an unfamiliar word, you can break the word into parts. This can help you recognize and pronounce it. You may find roots, prefixes, or suffixes.

A root is the base, or main part, of the word. It is the part of the word that has meaning by itself. A prefix goes in front of the root and changes the word's meaning.

For example, the description of South Asia you are going to read is a *nonfiction* text. The prefix *non-* means "not." *Fiction* describes stories that are imagined or make-believe. So the word *nonfiction* refers to text that tells about something that really happened (is not make-believe).

In this section, you will read the word *nonviolent*. Now that you know the meaning of the prefix *non-*, you can break *nonviolent* into a root and a prefix to figure out the word's meaning.

Vocabulary Strategy

Using Word Origins Many English words come from other languages. When you learn about the origins of words, you also learn about history. For example, you will read in this section that the British ruled India for many years. This is one way words from the Hindi language (spoken in India) entered the English language. You may be surprised to learn that *pajamas, shampoo, jungle,* and *bungalow* are all Hindi words.

Have you ever heard of a **cashmere** sweater? Cashmere is a very fine and expensive wool from goats that are raised in a region on the border of India and Pakistan. Read on to find out the name of this region. Think about how it relates to the word *cashmere*.

Section 1 Summary

New Religions

The Indus Valley, in present-day South Asia, was home to an early civilization. The civilization thrived for centuries. But by 1500 B.C. it was coming to an end.

About the same time, newcomers arrived in the region. They brought a new culture with them. Their culture then combined with the ancient languages and beliefs of the Indus Valley people. As a result, a new culture was created. The people who practiced this mixed culture were called Aryans (AYR ee unz).

The Aryans ruled northern India for more than 1,000 years. They divided people into four classes. The classes were 1) priests and the educated; 2) rulers and warriors; 3) farmers, artisans, and merchants; and 4) laborers. This division was called the **caste** system.

The caste system became part of a new religion founded in India, Hinduism. It is one of the world's oldest religions. Hindus worship many gods and goddesses. Each one stands for different parts of a single spirit. Today, Hinduism is the main religion of India. ✓

✓ Reading Check

Which ancient religion founded in India is the main religion there today?

____

____

Buddhism also developed in India. Buddhism is based on the idea that giving up selfish desires will free all people from pain. Buddhism spread to many parts of Asia. It spread to China, Tibet, Korea, and Japan. But it has almost died out in India.

From Empires to Nations

Look at the chart below to learn about three empires of ancient India.

Maurya Empire 321 B.C. to 185 B.C.	Gupta Empire A.D. 320 to A.D. 550	Mughal Empire 1556 to 1700s
• conquered many kingdoms • supported Buddhism • had laws for fair government	• strong central government • developed system of writing numerals • created temples and wall paintings	• introduced Islam • supported arts and literature

✓

✓ Reading Check

What are some contributions from the Gupta Empire?

____

____

____

Key Term

caste (kast) *n.* in the Hindu religion, a social group into which people are born and which they cannot change

In the late 1700s, much of the Indian subcontinent was ruled by the British. In 1858, India officially became a British **colony**.

In the early 1900s, the people of India wanted independence from Great Britain. An Indian leader named Mohandas K. Gandhi (GAHN dee) called for Indians to fight against British rule. But Gandhi wanted to fight in nonviolent ways. For example, he encouraged a **boycott** of British goods. Britain gave India its freedom in 1947.

Muslims in India were outnumbered by Hindus. They were afraid of losing their rights after independence. So they decided to fight for a separate state. Fighting led to a **partition** of the subcontinent into Pakistan and India in 1947. Most people in Pakistan were Muslims; most people in India were Hindus.

Since independence, Pakistan and India have fought for control of Kashmir (KASH mihr). Kashmir is an area on the border of India and Pakistan.

South Asian Cultures Today

History shapes South Asia's cultures. Hinduism and Islam are the major religions of South Asia today. About 80 percent of the people of India are Hindus. Hinduism is also the main religion of Nepal. Islam is the main religion of Pakistan and Bangladesh. ✓

Many languages are spoken in South Asia. India has 15 major languages. About 30 percent of Indians speak Hindi. English is also an official language there.

Review Questions

1. Which group of people developed the caste system?

____

2. What led to the partition of India in 1947?

____

Key Terms

colony (KAHL uh nee) *n.* a territory ruled by another nation
boycott (BOY kaht) *n.* a refusal to buy or use goods and services in order to show disapproval or to cause change
partition (pahr TISH un) *n.* a division into parts or portions

Target Reading Skill

Look for the word *subcontinent* in the bracketed paragraph. The prefix *sub-* means a smaller or less important part. What is the difference between a subcontinent and a continent?

____

Vocabulary Strategy

What is the name of the region that India and Pakistan have fought over since partition? (It is also known for a wool called cashmere.)

____

✓ Reading Check

In which two South Asian countries is Hinduism the main religion?

____

CHAPTER 5

Prepare to Read

Section 2
Southwest Asia: Cultures and History

Objectives

1. Find out that one of the world's earliest civilizations grew in Southwest Asia.
2. Understand that three of the world's great religions began in Southwest Asia.
3. Examine the different ethnic groups and religions of Southwest Asia.
4. Learn about the conflict between Arabs and Israelis in Southwest Asia.

Target Reading Skill

Analyze Word Parts Remember that a root is the base of a word. It has meaning by itself. A suffix comes at the end of a root and changes its meaning. A suffix may change the root's part of speech. For example, adding a suffix may change a verb into a noun.

In this section, you will read the word *creation*. The suffix *-ion* added to the root makes the new word a noun. If you know what the word *create* means, you can figure out the meaning of *creation*.

Vocabulary Strategy

Using Word Origins Many English words come from ancient Greek. Many words of Greek origin combine more than one root. Often a Greek word is the root of many words in English.

In this section you will read the word *monotheism*. Break it down for a closer look.

Greek Origin of *monotheism*

	prefix	root	suffix
Word Part	mono-	the	-ism
Greek Word	mono-	theo	-ismos
Meaning	one	god	belief in

Monotheism means "the belief in one god." Some other words that contain some of these Greek roots include *monogamy*, *monopoly*, *monotonous*, and *theology*. Can you think of any others?

Section 2 Summary

Mesopotamia

One of the world's earliest civilizations developed between the Tigris and Euphrates rivers. The region was called Mesopotamia, which means "between the rivers." It lies in present-day Iraq. ✓

The Mesopotamians developed a system of writing. They also had ideas about law that people use today. For example, they believed that all people must obey the same laws.

Birthplace of Three Religions

Three of the world's major religions began in Southwest Asia. They are Judaism, Christianity, and Islam.

Around 2000 B.C., Judaism was founded by Abraham. Abraham was a Mesopotamian who moved to Canaan, on the eastern shore of the Mediterranean Sea. Canaan later became known as Palestine. The Jews saw Palestine as their homeland.

Almost 2,000 years later, Jesus began preaching in Israel. Jesus was a Jew who traveled through Palestine. Christianity is based on the life and teachings of Jesus.

In about A.D. 600, the founder of Islam, Muhammad, began teaching in present-day Saudi Arabia. Today Islam is the largest religion in Southwest Asia. Five times a day, Muslims pray when called by a **muezzin**.

People who practice these three religions share a belief in **monotheism**. They worship the same God. He is known as Allah in Islam.

Major Religions Founded in Southwest Asia

	Judaism	Christianity	Islam
Birthplace	Palestine	Palestine	Saudi Arabia
Founded in	2000 B.C.	A.D. 30	A.D. 600
Founded by	Abraham	Jesus	Muhammad
Belief System	monotheism	monotheism	monotheism
Sacred Text	Torah	Bible (includes the Torah)	Quran
Followers	Jews	Christians	Muslims

✓

Key Terms

muezzin (myoo EZ in) *n.* a person whose job is to call Muslims to pray

monotheism (MAHN oh thee iz um) *n.* a belief that there is only one god

✓ Reading Check

In what present-day country did Mesopotamia develop?

Vocabulary Strategy

Monotheism is the belief in one god. *Poly-* means "many." What do you think the word *polytheism* means?

✓ Reading Check

Why is Southwest Asia considered the birthplace of Judaism, Christianity, and Islam?

Diverse Cultures in Southwest Asia

The people of Southwest Asia belong to a mix of ethnic groups. Arabic-speaking Arabs are the largest ethnic group in the region. Islam is the main religion. Non-Arab people live mainly in Israel, Turkey, and Iran. In Israel, most people are Jewish. Most people in Turkey are Turkish, but some are Kurdish. About half the people in Iran are Persian. ✓

✓ Reading Check

What is the main ethnic group in Israel?

______

______

______

Southwest Asia: Recent History

Before and during World War II, Nazi Germany killed more than six million European Jews just because they were Jewish. This is known as the **Holocaust**. Many Jews see Palestine as their homeland. But most were pushed out of the area in ancient times. Many Holocaust survivors migrated to Palestine. In 1948, Jews created a Jewish state, Israel.

Target Reading Skill

If to migrate means "move from one country or place to another," what is a *migration? Hint:* the suffix *-ion* added to the root made the new word a noun.

______

______

______

Arabs who lived in Palestine saw it as their homeland, too. So several Arab nations invaded Israel. Israel drove away the Arab forces. Since 1948, Israel and its Arab neighbors have fought several wars.

Israel and the Palestinians have worked towards peace. But conflict between the groups continues.

Another conflict in the area took place in Iraq. Iraq was defeated in the 1991 Persian Gulf War. But its leader, Saddam Hussein (suh DAHM hoo SAYN), refused to cooperate with the United Nations. In March 2003, U.S. forces attacked Iraq. Three weeks later, Saddam fell from power. American officials began working with Iraqi leaders to set up a democratic government. ✓

✓ Reading Check

Give one example of conflict in Southwest Asia

______

______

______

Review Questions

1. Describe Mesopotamia's location.

______

______

2. Which ethnic groups live in Southwest Asia today?

______

______

Key Term

Holocaust (HAHL uh kawst) *n.* the systematic killing of more than six million European Jews and others by Nazi Germany before and during World War II

CHAPTER 5

Prepare to Read

Section 3
Central Asia: Cultures and History

Objectives

1. Learn that many cultures and peoples influenced Central Asia in ancient times.
2. Discover how Central Asian nations became independent and why they are a focus of world interest.

Target Reading Skill

Recognize Word Origins The origin of a word is where the word comes from. The English language is full of words from other languages, such as Greek, Latin, and German. Some of these words are used in their original form. Often, they have changed over time. Sometimes, a foreign word or root is joined with English prefixes or suffixes. It then makes a new word.

In this section, you will read the word *government*. It contains the root word *govern*, which comes from the Latin word *gubernare*, meaning "to steer." In *government*, the suffix *-ment* means "act or process." Knowing a word's origin can help you better understand the word's meaning. Can you see how government is related to the process of "steering" a country?

Vocabulary Strategy

Using Word Origins In this section, you will read about five former Soviet republics in Central Asia. Before the breakup of the Soviet Union, they were Soviet Socialist Republics (which was usually abbreviated as SSR). They were called Kazakh SSR, Kirghiz (or Kyrgyz) SSR, Tajik SSR, Turkmen SSR, and Uzbek SSR. Each one was named for its main ethnic group.

When they became independent, they no longer wanted to be called Soviet Socialist Republics. They needed to find new names. To their south was Afghanistan. The suffix *-stan* comes from the Persian language. It means "place of" or "land." The former Soviet Socialist Republics of Central Asia took on this suffix and became Kazakhstan, Kyrgyzstan, Tajikistan, Turkmenistan, and Uzbekistan.

Section 3 Summary

Meeting Place of Empires

Central Asia is located between East Asia and Europe. It was a crossroads for trade caravans and armies. Over time, dozens of ethnic groups settled there. Each group brought new ideas and ways of living.

More than 2,000 years ago, the Silk Road linked China and Europe. For hundreds of years it brought Central Asia into contact with East Asia, Southwest Asia, and Europe. Along with goods, the traders exchanged ideas and inventions. Cities grew up at oases along the route.

The Silk Road brought wealth. It also brought invaders. Many groups of conquerors fought to control Central Asia. Some ruled for hundreds of years. But each group was replaced by new invaders.

Each conqueror left a mark on the region. For example, around A.D. 700, a Muslim empire spread across Central Asia. Many people started to practice Islam. Today, most people in the region are Muslims.

By the late 1200s, people stopped using the Silk Road as a main trade route. They used sea routes instead. But this did not stop foreign powers from trying to take over the region.

In the 1800s, Russia took over parts of Central Asia. Russia built railroads, factories, and large farms in the region. Some Russians moved in and brought new ways of life. But the lives of most people stayed the same. They practiced Islam and lived as nomadic herders.

In 1922, Russian Communists formed the Soviet Union. They extended their control over much of Central Asia. They divided the region into five republics.

The Soviets forced people to stop living as nomads. Instead, people had to work on **collective farms**. The farms didn't always produce enough food. About one million Central Asians starved to death during the 1930s. ✓

Key Term

collective farm (kuh LEK tiv farhm) *n.* in a Communist country, a large farm formed from many private farms collected into a single unit controlled by the government

✓ Reading Check

What was the result of collective farms that the Soviets in Central Asia set up?

____

____

____

The Soviets built new industries, schools, and hospitals. But they gave people few freedoms. They tried to do away with Muslim religion and culture.

In 1979, the Soviets invaded Afghanistan. Afghan forces fought the Soviets for years. The Soviets gave up and pulled out their troops in 1989. Then the Afghans fought each other for power. Eventually, a group known as the Taliban took control of most of the country.

After Independence

In 1991, the Soviet Union split up. The five Soviet republics in Central Asia became independent countries.

Each of the new countries named itself after its main ethnic group. The suffix *-stan* is a Persian word that means "place of" or "land." Kazakhstan means "place of the Kazakhs." The five countries, along with Afghanistan, are sometimes called "the Stans."

The new countries are different in many ways. The largest is Kazakhstan. It has important natural resources, such as oil and natural gas. The smallest is Tajikistan. It is in the mountains and is very poor. ✓

Since independence, the new countries have started governing themselves. Most are hurt by weak economies. Many people are jobless. There is not good health care or education, and both are hard to get.

But people are proud of their culture. They are teaching their children about their religion. And they are allowed to use their native languages in schools, books, and the news.

Review Questions

1. Where is Central Asia located?

____

____

____

2. Describe one way that Soviet rule affected Central Asia.

____

____

____

Vocabulary Strategy

Earlier in this chapter, you read about another country whose name ends in "*-stan.*" It is in South Asia. What country is it?

____

____

✓ Reading Check

Name two important natural resources of Kazakhstan?

1. ______________________________

2. ______________________________

Target Reading Skill

Find the word *governing* in the first sentence of the bracketed paragraph. Compare this word to the word *government*. Remember that both words come from a Latin word that means "to steer." How does the meaning of *governing* differ from the meaning of *government*?

____

____

____

Chapter 5 Assessment

1. Which of the following events in South Asia happened last?
   A. The Maurya Empire was founded.
   B. The Aryans came to northern India.
   C. India became a colony in the British Empire.
   D. During the Gupta Empire, mathematicians came up with the system of writing numerals that we use today.

2. When India was divided in 1947, the Muslim state that was created was called
   A. Kashmir.
   B. Afghanistan.
   C. Pakistan.
   D. Bangladesh.

3. People who practice Judaism, Christianity, and Islam share a belief in
   A. the caste system.
   B. monotheism.
   C. many gods.
   D. Buddha.

4. The largest religion in Southwest Asia today is
   A. Hinduism.
   B. Buddhism.
   C. Judaism.
   D. Islam.

5. What was one result of the formation of the Soviet Union in 1922?
   A. The Soviets encouraged the growth of Islam in Central Asia.
   B. Central Asia was divided into five republics.
   C. Food production in Central Asia increased.
   D. More people in Central Asia lived as nomads.

Short Answer Question

What impact did the Silk Road have on Central Asia?

Chapter 6

Prepare to Read

Section 1
Southeast Asia: Cultures and History

Objectives

1. Find out why Southeast Asia is a culturally diverse region.
2. Learn how colonial powers affected Southeast Asia.
3. Understand how years of conflict affected Vietnam, Cambodia, and Laos.

Target Reading Skill

Understand Sequence A sequence is the order in which a series of events takes place. A timeline is a useful tool for keeping track of sequence.

A timeline represents a period of years. The earliest date is marked on the left end of the timeline, and the latest date is marked on the right end. The timeline below represents the years from 1900 to 2000. Notice how an event has been included in the timeline.

As you read, list important events on a timeline to help you remember what you have learned.

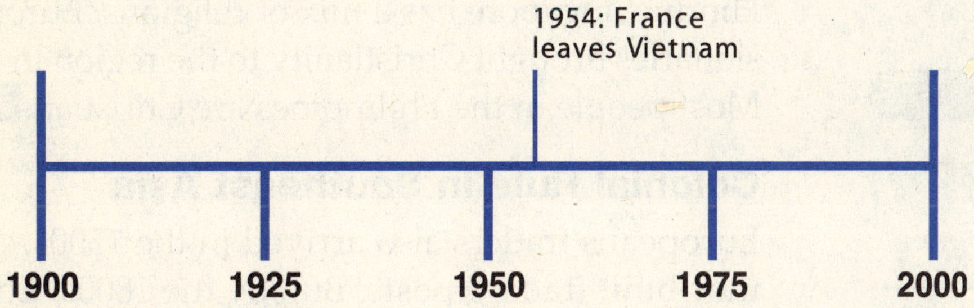

Vocabulary Strategy

Using Context Clues to Determine Meaning Many English words have more than one meaning. You can use context clues to figure out the meaning of a word. For example, in the sentences below, the word *back* is used in two different ways.

He wrote his answers on the **back** of the worksheet.

By using context clues, you can figure out that in this sentence, *back* means "reverse side."

She asked her friends to **back** her plan.

Context clues tell you that in this sentence, *back* means "support."

Section 1 Summary

The **Khmer Empire** was at its height from about A.D. 800 to 1434. It was one of many kingdoms in Southeast Asia.

A Region of Diversity

For a long time, Southeast Asia's mountains kept groups of people apart. As a result, each group had its own way of life. Eventually, Southeast Asia came into contact with its neighbors, India and China. They soon had a strong effect on the cultures of Southeast Asia.

Indian traders sailed across the Indian Ocean to Southeast Asia over 2,000 years ago. Indians brought the religions of Hinduism and Buddhism to the region. Later, Muslim traders from northern India brought Islam to Indonesia and the Philippines.

In 111 B.C., China conquered Vietnam. It ruled the country for more than 1,000 years. The Vietnamese adopted Chinese ways of farming and government.

Today, most people in Myanmar, Thailand, Laos, Vietnam, and Cambodia are Buddhist. Most people in Malaysia and Indonesia are Muslim, and some are Hindu. Singapore has a mix of religions. European missionaries brought Christianity to the region in the 1500s. Most people in the Philippines are Christian. ✓

Colonial Rule in Southeast Asia

Europeans traders also arrived in the 1500s. At first, they built trading posts. But, by the 1800s, European nations controlled most of Southeast Asia. Thailand was the only country in Southeast Asia that was not under colonial rule by 1914. ✓

Spain ruled the Philippines for about 350 years. In 1898, the United States won the Spanish-American War, taking control of the Philippines.

The colonial rulers in Southeast Asia built roads, bridges, ports, and railroads. This helped the economies of the colonies. People and goods could move around more. The colonial rulers also built schools.

Key Term

Khmer Empire (kuh MEHR EM pyr) *n.* an empire that included much of present-day Cambodia, Thailand, Malaysia, and part of Laos

Vocabulary Strategy

The word *height* has several meanings. You may already know one of its meanings. What is its meaning in this context? You may want to consult a dictionary.

____

____

____

✓ Reading Check

List four religions practiced in Southeast Asia.

1. ______________________
2. ______________________
3. ______________________
4. ______________________

✓ Reading Check

Which country in Southeast Asia was not under colonial rule by 1914?

Country: ____________________

By the early 1900s, **nationalists** in Southeast Asia were working to gain independence for their countries. During World War II, the Japanese invaded Southeast Asia and forced the European powers out. After the war, Southeast Asian countries did gain independence.

Vietnam, Cambodia, and Laos

Laos, Cambodia, and Vietnam were French colonies before World War II. Together, they were known as French Indochina. After the war, France tried to regain control of them. Nationalist forces in Vietnam fought against the French. In 1954, the French gave up and left.

[In 1954, Vietnam was divided in two. North Vietnam was Communist. South Vietnam was non-Communist. Leaders in North Vietnam wanted one country under Communist rule. They invaded South Vietnam. South Vietnam fought back with help from the United States.]

After years of fighting, the United States withdrew its forces. In 1975, North Vietnam took over South Vietnam. The reunited country was Communist. ✓

Cambodia and Laos became independent from France in 1953. As in Vietnam, Communists and non-Communists struggled for power.

In 1975, Cambodia's Communist party, the **Khmer Rouge**, took over the government of Cambodia. The Khmer Rouge had brutal policies. It killed more than a million Cambodians. Cambodia held elections in 1998 that put a new government in place. The new government worked to make Cambodia safe and free.

Target Reading Skill

Read the bracketed paragraph. When did Vietnam split into two countries?

____

✓ Reading Check

Which country did the United States support with troops during the Vietnam War?

____

____

Review Questions

1. Which two Asian countries neighbor Southeast Asia?

____

____

2. Which colonies did French Indochina include?

____

____

Key Terms

nationalist (NASH uh nul ist) *n.* a person who is devoted to the interests of his or her country

Khmer Rouge (kuh MEHR roozh) *n.* the Cambodian Communist party

CHAPTER 6

Prepare to Read

Section 2
The Pacific Region: Cultures and History

Objectives

1. Find out how people settled Australia and New Zealand.
2. Learn which groups shaped the cultures of Australia and New Zealand.
3. Understand how Pacific island nations have been affected by other cultures.

Target Reading Skill

Recognize Signal Words Signal words are words or phrases that prepare you for what is coming next. They are like the directions in a recipe for baking a cake. When baking, you need to know when to add the ingredients, how long to mix or bake, and when to ask an adult to take something out of the oven.

When you read, look for words such as *first*, *before*, *later*, *next*, and *recently*. They signal the order in which events took place.

Vocabulary Strategy

Using Context to Clarify Meaning Sometimes you may read a word you recognize, but you aren't sure about its meaning. Many words have more than one meaning. What a word means depends on its context. Look for clues in the surrounding words or sentences. For example, the word *standard* has many meanings. You will find out which meaning the author had in mind by looking at the context.

Some examples of *standard* are listed below.

Word	Definitions	Examples
standard	a flag or banner	The winners raised their standard in the air.
	something used as a basis for comparison	The government set standards for clean air.
	something used as a base or support	The flag was attached to a standard.
	a piece of music that remains popular through the years	She has released a CD of old standards.

Section 2 Summary

Settlement

The first people in New Zealand were the **Maori**. They had traveled from Asia to Polynesia. Then, about 1,000 years ago, the Maori sailed to New Zealand.

The first settlers in Australia were the **Aborigines**. Many scientists think that the Aborigines traveled from Asia to Australia more than 40,000 years ago. For thousands of years, they moved from place to place, hunting and gathering food. People lived in small family groups. They had strong religious beliefs about nature and the land.

In 1788, the British founded the first colony in Australia. It was a **penal colony**. Other colonists soon settled there. Then, in 1851, gold was found. The population soared. In 1901, Australia gained its independence. ✓

The British settled New Zealand at about the same time as Australia. The colony had good harbors and fertile soil. It attracted many British settlers. It gained independence in 1947.

The Cultures of Australia and New Zealand

Most Australians and New Zealanders are descendants of British settlers. They share British culture and customs. Most have a high standard of living. ✓

Since the arrival of Europeans, the Aborigines have suffered hardships. Settlers forced them off their lands. Thousands died of European diseases. Others were forced to work on sheep and cattle **stations**. Even their children were taken from them to grow up with non-Aborigines. Today, Aborigines make up less than 1 percent of the population.

Key Terms

Maori (MAH oh ree) *n.* a native of New Zealand whose ancestors first traveled from Asia to Polynesia, and later to New Zealand

Aborigine (ab uh RIJ uh nee) *n.* a member of the earliest people of Australia, who probably came from Asia

penal colony (PEEN ul KAHL uh nee) *n.* a place where people convicted of crimes are sent

station (STAY shun) *n.* in Australia, a large ranch for raising livestock

Target Reading Skill

In the paragraph at the left, circle the words that signal when and how the Maori came to New Zealand.

Mark the Text

✓ Reading Check

What happened after gold was found in Australia?

Vocabulary Strategy

In the bracketed paragraph, how is the word *standard* used? Copy the correct definition from the chart at the beginning of this section.

Mark the Text

✓ Reading Check

Why do most Australians and New Zealanders share British culture and customs?

Non-British people also settled in Australia. Many came during the gold rush, including the Chinese. Almost 3 percent of Australia's population is Chinese.

When New Zealand became a British colony, Britain promised to protect Maori land. But settlers broke that promise. For many years, the Maori and the settlers fought. The settlers won. The Maori were forced to adopt English ways. Now, the Maori can practice their culture. About 15 percent of New Zealand's people are Maori. Their culture is important to New Zealand life.

After World War II, many Europeans migrated to New Zealand. People from Polynesia have also settled there. New Zealand's largest city, Auckland, has more Polynesians than any other city in the world.

The Cultures of the Pacific Islands

Scientists believe the first people to live on the Pacific islands were settlers from Southeast Asia. They came to the Pacific islands more than 30,000 years ago. First, they settled on the island of New Guinea.

The island groups were too far apart for people to stay in touch. Each group developed its own language, customs, and religious beliefs. But they did have much in common. They got their food from the ocean. They also used the ocean for travel and trade.

In the 1800s, Western nations began to move into the Pacific islands. By 1900, the United States, Britain, France, and Germany had claimed nearly every island.

After World War II, most of the islands gained independence. By then, traditional cultures had blended with other cultures. Most had democratic governments. Many Pacific islanders read and spoke English. ✓

✓ Reading Check

What were Pacific island cultures like after World War II?

____

____

____

Review Questions

1. In what ways were the histories of the Aborigines and the Maori similar?

____

____

2. From where do scientists believe the first people to live in the Pacific islands came?

____

____

Chapter 6 Assessment

1. Which two countries had a strong influence on Southeast Asian cultures?
   A. India and Britain
   B. China and India
   C. India and France
   D. China and Japan

2. What happened after the Khmer Rouge took over the government of Cambodia?
   A. Cambodia became a democratic country.
   B. People in Cambodia were able to live freely and peacefully.
   C. Cambodia finally gained independence from France.
   D. The government killed more than a million Cambodians.

3. The first colony in Australia was set up by
   A. Great Britain.
   B. the United States.
   C. India.
   D. France.

4. Besides the British settlers, many people from ________________ came to Australia during the gold rush.
   A. Cambodia
   B. India
   C. China
   D. Laos

5. After World War II, most Pacific islands gained
   A. independence.
   B. their own colonies.
   C. additional land.
   D. membership in the European Union.

Short Answer Question

How did communism affect Southeast Asia starting in the 1950s?

____

____

____

____

CHAPTER 7

Prepare to Read

Section 1
China: Transforming Itself

Objectives

1. Find out how China controlled its economy from 1949 to 1980.
2. Learn about the growth of Taiwan since 1949.
3. Discover how China's government operated after the death of Mao Zedong.
4. Examine aspects of life in China today.

Target Reading Skill

Compare and Contrast When you compare, you look for the way two things are alike. When you contrast, you look at how two things are different. For example, in this section, you will notice that the "two Chinas"—China and Taiwan—are alike because the people of both countries are Chinese. On the other hand, each country has a different form of government and a different economic system.

Comparing and contrasting is another way to process information and understand what you read.

Vocabulary Strategy

Recognizing Word Usage The Chinese use a completely different writing system than the alphabet used in English. Their system uses symbols for words. In English, the alphabet uses symbols for sounds. For example, in Chinese characters, China's first Communist leader's name is 毛澤東. As you can see, you cannot read the name unless you can read Chinese characters. So that westerners can read Chinese names, there is also a system of spelling called Pinyin. Pinyin means "join together sounds." In Pinyin, the first Communist leader's name is Mao Zedong. The Chinese government uses Pinyin when it sends printed news releases to the Western world.

Section 1 Summary

China's Economy, 1949–1980

In 1949, the Chinese Communist party set up a new government. Mao Zedong (mow dzuh doong) was in charge. The government took over China's factories, businesses, and farmland. In 1958, Mao began a **radical** program. It was called the "Great Leap Forward." It was supposed to help farms and factories produce more goods. Unfortunately, many factories made low-quality or useless products. ✓

✓ Reading Check

What was the purpose of China's Great Leap Forward?

____

____

____

At the same time, poor weather destroyed crops. There was not enough food. Between 1959 and 1961, as many as 30 million people starved to death.

In 1966, Mao introduced another radical plan, the Cultural Revolution. He wanted to create a new society. Mao encouraged students to rebel and to join the **Red Guards**. Mao's Red Guards destroyed some of China's ancient buildings. They put artists and teachers in jail. When the Cultural Revolution ended in 1976, hundreds of thousands of people were dead.

Taiwan Since 1949

Taiwan is an island southeast of mainland China. The Nationalists had fought the Communists for control of China after World War II. The Communists won in 1949. The Nationalists fled to Taiwan and formed their own country, the Republic of China.

The Nationalists used the **free enterprise system**. Even in the 1950s, Taiwan's economy was one of Asia's strongest. The government there started programs that helped farms produce more crops, which helped Taiwan make more money. ✓

✓ Reading Check

What kind of economic system did the nationalists in Taiwan use?

____

____

____

Both Taiwan and China claimed to be the "real" China. Each wanted to rule the other. At first, Western countries supported Taiwan.

Key Terms

radical (RAD ih kul) *adj.* extreme

Red Guards (red gahrdz) *n.* groups of students who carried out Mao Zedong's policies during the Cultural Revolution

free enterprise system (free ENT ur pryz SIS tum) *n.* an economic system in which people can choose their own jobs, start private businesses, own property, and make a profit

Target Reading Skill

Read the paragraphs under the heading "Changes in China." List three ways China was different after Mao Zedong died.

1. ____________________

2. ____________________

3. ____________________

Vocabulary Strategy

A name in the bracketed paragraph is spelled using Pinyin. Find and circle the name.

Mark the Text

✓ Reading Check

What happened to Hong Kong in 1997?

____

____

____

✓ Reading Check

How did China's government respond to demands for democracy in 1989?

____

____

____

Changes in China

Many Western countries would not trade with China. At the same time, some of Mao's policies hurt the country. In the 1970s, the Communists began to see that they needed to change their policies.

First, China began to fix relations with the West. In 1971, it joined the United Nations. In 1972, Richard Nixon was the first American president to visit China. The two nations began to trade.

Mao died in 1976. The new leader, Deng Xiaoping (dung show ping), started a program, The Four Modernizations, to improve farming, industry, science, and defense.

Deng allowed some foreign companies to own businesses. He allowed some Chinese citizens to run private businesses. By 2000, private businesses produced about 75 percent of China's **gross domestic product**.

In 1997, China took back control of Hong Kong, which had been a British colony since the late 1800s. It was a major center for trade, banking, and shipping. ✓

China Today

China is now a major economic power. But the government has been criticized for the way it treats its people. People who want a democratic government are sometimes put in prison, wounded, or killed. In 1989, the government killed and wounded thousands of people demanding democracy in Beijing's Tiananmen Square. ✓

In 2003, Hu Jintao became China's president. Hu may loosen government control over the economy.

Review Questions

1. Who took control of China in 1949?

____

____

2. Where is the Republic of China?

____

____

Key Term

gross domestic product (grohs duh MES tik PRAHD ukt) *n.* the total value of all goods and services produced in an economy

CHAPTER 7

Prepare to Read

Section 2
Japan: Tradition and Change

Objectives

1. Learn about the growth of Japan's economy.
2. Find out about successes and challenges in Japan's economy.
3. Examine aspects of life in Japan.

Target Reading Skill

Make Comparisons When you compare you look for the way two things are alike. It is often easier to understand new facts by comparing them with facts you already know. For example, which of the following facts is easier to understand?

> Japan has a total area of 145,841 square miles (377,727 square kilometers).
>
> Japan is slightly smaller than California.

Most people would choose the second fact. It can be hard to picture the actual size of a place you don't know. But when it is compared to a place you do know, such as California, you can probably picture it much better.

Vocabulary Strategy

Recognizing Word Usage There are two ways that people who use the English language shorten words to save time or space. One way is by using abbreviations. Another is by using brief forms. Brief forms are shortened forms of words.

Some common brief forms include *auto* (for *automobile*), *sub* (for *submarine*), *mike* (for *microphone*), and *phone* (for *telephone*).

Often, the brief form becomes much more common than the full form. For example, *fax* is used more often than its full form, *facsimile*. In fact, many people probably don't even realize that *fax* is a brief form!

In this chapter, you will read the word *stereo*. Did you know that it is a brief form for *stereophonic*? It can refer either to a small listening device or to a large sound system.

What other brief forms can you think of?

Section 2 Summary

Building a Developed Economy

In the early 1900s, the Japanese worked to build their industries. By the 1920s, Japan was an important manufacturing country.

World War II left Japan in ruins. The United States helped rebuild its industries. Also, the Japanese government helped rebuild by giving **subsidies** to industries. Companies built large factories and sold more goods.

High-technology industries are an important part of Japan's economy. Japan produces industrial robots, watches, and cameras. Japan builds and sells cars and produces huge amounts of steel, ships, televisions, bicycles, and compact discs (CDs).

Japanese companies also made existing products better. The videocassette recorder (VCR) was invented in the United States. But it cost too much to make there. A Japanese company bought the invention. Now Japan is a leading maker of VCRs.

Japanese companies also invented many new things, such as small electronic games you hold in your hand. Also, a Japanese company and European company together made the first CD. The Japanese also helped create the digital video disc (DVD). ☑

Successes and Challenges

In the 1980s, Japan had one of the largest and strongest economies in the world. Its economy depended on selling its products to America and Europe. But the Japanese did not buy many goods from America and Europe.

This situation hurt Japan's trade relationship with other countries. Then, in the early 1990s, there was a **recession** in Japan. The economy made less money. Some companies began to lay off workers. ☑

Key Terms

subsidy (SUB suh dee) *n.* money given by a government to assist a private company

recession (rih SESH un) *n.* a period during which an economy and the businesses that support it make less money

Vocabulary Strategy

What is the brief form for bicycle?

____

____

✓ Reading Check

Name two high-technology products made in Japan.

1. ______________________

2. ______________________

✓ Reading Check

How was Japan affected by the recession in the 1990s?

____

____

____

Despite these problems, Japan still has one of the largest economies in the world. Manufacturing is still important. But now, more people work in Japan's service industries than in manufacturing. Service industries include banking, communications, sales, hotels, and restaurants.

Life in Japan

Life in Japan today is a mix of traditional values and modern changes. One Japanese tradition is working together as a group. For example, companies form *keiretsu* (kay ret soo). Keiretsu is a group of companies that work toward one another's success. A keiretsu may include different kinds of companies—some that make goods, some that provide raw materials for the goods, and some that sell the goods.

The tradition of marriage is changing. Today, many Japanese are choosing not to marry or to get married later. As a result, the **birthrate** is low.

Before World War II, few women in Japan worked outside the home. Today, more women work than stay home. And half the people who work are women.

Today, Japan needs more workers. Because of the low birthrate, Japan does not have enough young workers. At the same time, the number of older people who can no longer work is growing. With a smaller **labor** force, or fewer workers available, companies must pay more to attract workers. This increases the cost of the goods and services they produce. ✓

Review Questions

1. Describe Japan's role in the high-technology industry.

____

____

2. Why does Japan not have enough workers?

____

____

Key Terms

birthrate (BURTH rayt) *n.* the number of live births each year per 1,000 people

labor (LAY bur) *n.* the work people do for which they are paid

Target Reading Skill

In the bracketed paragraphs, find one Japanese tradition that has remained the same and one tradition that has changed.

____

____

____

✓ Reading Check

What happens when there are fewer workers available?

____

____

____

CHAPTER 7

Prepare to Read

Section 3
The Koreas: A Divided Land

Objectives

1. Understand why North Korea has been slow to develop.
2. Find out how South Korea became an economic success.

Target Reading Skill

Identify Contrasts Suppose that on a warm sunny day, you stepped into an air-conditioned movie theater. The temperature and lighting inside the theater would be completely different from those outside. You would notice the contrast right away.

It is a little more difficult to notice contrasts when you read. But it is an important skill. Sometimes two things are contrasted in the same sentence. Sometimes the contrast is in different paragraphs, and sometimes it is under different headings. A chart is a good way to keep track of contrasts.

Use a chart like the one below to keep track of the differences between North Korea and South Korea.

North Korea	South Korea
• Low economic growth	• High economic growth
• Low industrial growth	• High industrial growth

Vocabulary Strategy

Recognizing Word Usage As you read, you will often see abbreviations used in place of full terms. Abbreviations save space and time. An abbreviation may be a shortened form of a word. For example, *Mr.* is an abbreviation for *Mister*. Many abbreviations are made up of initials, as in *NY* for *New York*.

You already know that *USA* is the abbreviation for *United States of America* and that *UN* is the abbreviation for *United Nations*. Other common abbreviations for country names include *UK* (*United Kingdom*) and *USSR* (*Union of Soviet Socialist Republics*).

In this section, you will see the abbreviation *DMZ*. Read the next page to find out what it stands for.

Section 3 Summary

The border between North Korea and South Korea is not like any other in the world. It runs through the **demilitarized zone**, or DMZ. The DMZ is about 2.5 miles (4 kilometers) wide and about 151 miles (248 kilometers) long. Weapons and defenses line both sides.

North Korea has an estimated one million troops at the border. South Korea has about 600,000 troops. Why does the DMZ exist? In 1953, a **truce** ended the Korean War. But no peace treaty was signed. Since then, the border dividing the two countries has been defended by military more heavily than any other border.

More than the DMZ divides the Koreas. There are many differences between the two countries.

North Korea: Economic Challenges

North Korea is a communist country, under a dictatorship. The government runs the economy. The country has shut itself off to much of the world. It has kept out new technology and ideas. But it has rich mineral resources. Until the end of World War II, it was Korea's industrial center.

Today, it cannot compete with South Korea. It makes poor goods in government-owned factories. The government has done little to **diversify** the economy. The economy is in bad shape.

Farming methods are also outdated in North Korea. Many farmers burn hillsides to get ready to plant crops. After a few years of this, rain washes the good soil away. Then fields can no longer be farmed. In 1995, North Korea faced **famine**. Officials estimated that 220,000 people starved to death between 1995 and 1998. For the first time, North Korea asked noncommunist countries for help. ☑

Key Terms

demilitarized zone (dee MIL uh tuh ryzd zohn) *n.* an area in which no weapons are allowed
truce (troos) *n.* an agreement to end fighting
diversify (duh VUR suh fy) *v.* to add variety to
famine (FAM in) *n.* a huge food shortage

Vocabulary Strategy

What does the abbreviation *DMZ* stand for?

✓ Reading Check

How did famine affect North Korea?

Target Reading Skill

How is North Korea's government different from South Korea's government?

____

____

____

✓ Reading Check

Name three products made in South Korea.

1. ______________________
2. ______________________
3. ______________________

✓ Reading Check

What happened when North Korea announced it was developing nuclear weapons?

____

____

____

South Korea: Economic Growth

In the mid-1950s, South Korea had few industries. Now it has a strong economy.

South Korea is a democracy. Its economy is based on free enterprise. After World War II, its factories made cloth and processed foods. Today, South Korea produces many different kinds of goods. These include ships, electronics, and silicon chips. South Korea also processes oil to make plastics, rubber, and other goods. ✓

South Korea's government has helped industry grow. And it has helped farmers. Some of its programs helped farmers produce more crops. Other programs helped improve housing, roads, and water supplies.

As successful as South Korea is, it does face some challenges. For example, it does not have many natural resources. It must bring in raw materials from other countries to keep industry running.

Years of Tension

The two Koreas have had a tense relationship since the end of the Korean War. There have been many clashes between their troops. In 2000, the leaders of the two countries agreed to work toward peace and cooperation.

But in 2002, North Korea announced that it had been developing nuclear weapons. The news hurt hopes for peace between the two countries. It caused great concern all over the world. The United States, South Korea, and Japan called for North Korea to stop its nuclear weapons program. ✓

Review Questions

1. Why is North Korea's economy less successful than South Korea's?

____

____

____

2. How did the relationship between North Korea and South Korea improve in 2000?

____

____

____

Chapter 7 Assessment

1. The goal of China's Great Leap Forward was to
   A. build backyard furnaces for making steel.
   B. take farmers away from farming the land.
   C. help farms and factories produce more goods.
   D. release businesses and farms from government control.

2. After 1976, Chinese leaders such as Deng Xiaoping began to change China's economy by
   A. tightening government control over industry.
   B. focusing on improvements in farming, industry, science, and defense.
   C. not allowing free enterprise.
   D. limiting political freedom.

3. Japan has
   A. communes.
   B. a high birthrate.
   C. a growing labor force.
   D. a successful economy.

4. How are the governments of China and North Korea similar?
   A. They are both ruled by kings.
   B. They both have communist governments.
   C. They both use the free enterprise system.
   D. They both have democratic governments.

5. Which is NOT true of South Korea?
   A. It is a democracy.
   B. Its economy is strong.
   C. The government has improved housing and roads.
   D. It has all the raw materials it needs for industry.

Short Answer Question

What was the purpose of the Cultural Revolution?

____

____

____

____

CHAPTER 8

Prepare to Read

Section 1
India: In the Midst of Change

Objectives

1. Learn about key features of India's population.
2. Examine the state of India's economy.
3. Understand major challenges facing India.

Target Reading Skill

Identify Causes and Effects A cause makes something happen. An effect is what happens. It is the result of the cause. As you read, pause to ask yourself, "What happened or is going to happen?" The answer to that question is the effect. Then ask yourself, "Why is this happening?" The answer to that question is the cause. Practice using this example.

India has more than one billion people. And its population is growing. By 2050, India is expected to have more people than any other country.

Ask yourself, "What is going to happen?" The answer—India is going to have more people than any other country—is the effect. Now ask yourself, "Why is that going to happen?" The answer—because the population is growing—is the cause.

Vocabulary Strategy

Recognizing Roots A root is a base word that has meaning by itself. Many words have a few letters attached to the beginning or the end of a root to make another word. These added letters change the meaning of the base word. The table below shows examples of words that are made from attaching letters to different roots.

Attached Letters	Root	New Word
un-	clear	unclear
-ing	do	doing

When you come across a new word, see if it contains a root that you already know. You can use the root to help you figure out what the word means.

Section 1 Summary

Key Features of India's Population

Right now, China has more people than any other country in the world. India is second. India has more than one billion people. And its population is growing. By 2050, India is expected to have more people than any other country in the world.

About 72 percent of India's people live in the countryside, but nearly 300 million people live in cities. By 2030, more than 600 million will be living in cities. That's about the same as all the people who live in the United States, Brazil, and Russia together. ✓

About one fourth of India's people live in poverty. That means that they make just enough money to buy the food they need to live and nothing else. Recently, though, the middle class has been growing. People in the middle class make enough money to buy goods and services that make their lives better. India's middle class may be one of the largest in the world.

A Growing Economy

India's economy is growing quickly. In the early 1990s, India's democratic government made it easier for companies from other countries to do business in India. The middle class helps the economy, too. Middle class people buy many of the goods and services made in India. This keeps money in India and helps businesses grow. As the middle class grows, the number of poor people should shrink.

Growing industries also help India's economy. Computer software programming is a major industry that employs many highly educated and skilled workers. India also produces large quantities of other products, such as electrical appliances. And India produces more movies than any other country. ✓

India buys more than it sells. But it can produce all its own food. India sells **textiles**, gemstones, and jewelry. The United States is one of India's biggest customers.

Key Term

textiles (TEKS tylz) *n.* cloth made by weaving or by knitting

Vocabulary Strategy

The words listed below appear on this page. Each of these words contains another word that is its root. Underline the roots in the text as you read.

Mark the Text

growing
government
programming
electrical

Did knowing the root help you figure out the meaning of the words?

✓ Reading Check

List two facts about India's population.

1. ______________________

2. ______________________

✓ Reading Check

Name two major industries in India.

1. ______________________

2. ______________________

Target Reading Skill

Look at the bracketed paragraph to find two effects a growing population can have on a country.

1. ______________________

2. ______________________

✓ Reading Check

How has India improved health care for its people?

____

Progress and Challenges

For many years, India and Pakistan have fought over Kashmir. Kashmir is an area of land on the northern borders of India and Pakistan. The two countries have tried to settle the disagreement over Kashmir. But violence continues.

[India's biggest challenge will be taking care of its growing population. Each year more people will need jobs, housing, health care, and education. They will also need food, water, and electricity.]

Disease and **malnutrition** are problems for millions of Indians now. But these problems are slowly getting better. The government has taken steps to improve health care. It is paying for more doctors to work in rural areas. There are also programs to protect people from certain diseases. ☑

As a result, people in India are living longer. The average **life expectancy** was 53 years in 1981. In 2003, it was 63 years. This is an important measure of how well a country is caring for its citizens.

Another way of measuring how well a country is doing is the **literacy rate**. In 1991, just over 50 percent of Indians could read and write. In 2001, the rate had gone up to 65 percent. As education improves, the literacy rate will keep going up.

Review Questions

1. How does the middle class help India's economy?

____

2. Why is life expectancy increasing in India?

____

Key Terms

malnutrition (mal noo TRISH un) *n.* poor nutrition caused by a lack of food or an unbalanced diet

life expectancy (lyf ek SPEK tun see) *n.* the average number of years a person is expected to live

literacy rate (LIT ur uh see rayt) *n.* the percentage of a population age 15 and over that can read and write

CHAPTER 8

Prepare to Read

Section 2
Pakistan: An Economy Based on Agriculture

Objectives

1. Find out that Pakistan's economy is based on agriculture.
2. Learn about Pakistan's industries.

Target Reading Skill

Understand Effects Remember that a cause makes something happen. The effect is what happens as a result of the cause. One cause can have more than one effect.

As you read this section, look for the effects of Pakistan's water supply on its economy. Write the effects in a chart like the one below.

CAUSE	→	EFFECTS
• Water is in short supply in Pakistan.	→	• Farmers use canals to carry water to their fields. •

Vocabulary Strategy

Recognizing Roots Remember that a root is the base of a word that has meaning by itself. When groups of letters are added to a root word, they make a new word with a different meaning. But the meaning is still related to the root. There are many groups of letters that can be attached to roots to make new words. The table below shows some common examples.

Attached Letters	Root	New Word
non-	stop	nonstop
-ern	west	western
-ly	large	largely

When you come across an unfamiliar word, look at it closely. See if you can use its root to help you figure out what the word means.

Vocabulary Strategy

The words listed below appear on this page. Each of these words contains a group of letters that you have learned about attached to a root. Underline the root within each of these words.

melting
northern
mostly

How does the root help you figure out the meaning of these words?

✓ Reading Check

Why does most of Pakistan's farming take place in the Indus River basin?

____

____

____

Target Reading Skill

In the bracketed paragraph, look for three effects of Pakistan's use of canals and ditches for irrigation.

Effect 1. ______________________

____

Effect 2. ______________________

____

Effect 3. ______________________

____

Section 2 Summary

Pakistan does not get much rain. The country's water supply comes from three main sources: the Indus River, monsoon rains, and slow-melting glaciers. Pakistan needs to make good use of the little water it does get. To do this, it has built the world's largest irrigation system.

In 2001, Pakistan was in the middle of a terrible **drought**. The government was worried about the lack of water. It even thought about melting part of the glaciers in northern Pakistan to get water. They decided against it because they worried about hurting the environment.

An Agricultural Nation

Pakistan's economy is based mostly on agriculture, or farming. That is why water is so important.

Most of Pakistan's farming takes place in the Indus River basin. That is where the irrigation system is. Farmers grow cotton, wheat, sugar cane, and rice. Pakistan is one of the top ten cotton producers in the world. It grows so much rice it can sell it to other countries. ✓

Wheat is the major food crop in Pakistan. The **Green Revolution** has helped farmers there grow more wheat. The program helped by spreading modern farming methods and special kinds of grain. In 2000, Pakistan finally grew enough wheat to feed its people and still sell some to Afghanistan. One of Pakistan's major goals is to become **self-sufficient** in wheat production.

[Pakistan's farmers use thousands of canals and ditches to move water from the Indus River and its **tributaries** to their fields. This gives them a steady flow of water, even when there is no rainfall. As a result, more land can be farmed and more crops are produced.]

Key Terms

drought (drowt) *n.* a long period of dry weather
Green Revolution (green rev uh LOO shun) *n.* a worldwide effort to increase food production in developing countries
self-sufficient (self suh FISH unt) *adj.* able to supply one's own needs without any outside assistance
tributary (TRIB yoo tehr ee) *n.* a river that flows into a larger river

Irrigation solves many problems, but it creates others. For example, river water has salt in it. When crops are watered with river water, the salt ends up in the soil. This salty soil makes plants grow more slowly. As a result, Pakistani scientists are now looking for ways to help wheat grow in salty soil.

Another water problem in Pakistan is flooding. Heavy monsoon rains are to blame. The government has built dams to catch these rains. The water is then let into irrigation canals when needed.

Industry in Pakistan

Dams help both farmers and industries. Dams use the power of rushing water to make electricity. This hydroelectricity runs factories. Most of Pakistan's industry is located on the Indus River near sources of hydroelectric power.

Pakistan's industrial growth began with agriculture, because that is what the people knew best. Industries used crops that Pakistanis had grown for a long time, such as cotton. Today, Pakistan's economy depends largely on the textile industry. Textiles are cloth products made by weaving or knitting. Pakistan's textile products include cotton yarn and clothing. More than 60 percent of what Pakistan sells to other countries is made by the textile industry. ☑

There are also other industries. The chemical industry makes a variety of products. There are also several steel mills. They allow Pakistan to make most of the steel it needs. Making steel is cheaper than buying it from other countries.

Millions of Pakistanis work in small workshops instead of large factories. They make field hockey sticks, furniture, knives, and saddles, as well as beautiful carpets that are famous all over the world.

✓ Reading Check

Give one example of an industry in Pakistan based on agriculture.

____

____

Review Questions

1. Explain one bad result of irrigation in Pakistan.

____

____

2. How does Pakistan's textile industry help the country's economy?

____

____

CHAPTER 8

Prepare to Read

Section 3
Israel: Economics and Cultures

Objectives

1. Discover how Israel's economy has grown and changed over the years.
2. Learn about the different peoples living in Israel.

Target Reading Skill

Recognize Multiple Causes A cause makes something happen. An effect is what happens. Often, an effect can have more than one cause. For example, in this section, you will read about disagreements between the Israelis and the Palestinians. As you read this section, identify two causes for these disagreements.

Looking for more than one cause will help you fully understand why something happened. As you read this section, look for other things that have multiple causes.

Vocabulary Strategy

Using Roots and Suffixes A suffix is one or more syllables attached to the end of a word to make a new word. The word it is attached to is known as the root. When a suffix is added to a root, the new word has a new meaning.

Some common suffixes are listed below, along with their meanings and examples. Notice that some have more than one meaning. Learning to identify suffixes and their meanings will help you understand what you read.

Suffix	Meaning	Example
-ery	the practice of; the behavior or condition of	robbery, pottery, poverty
-ing	an action; result of an action	trying, drawing
-ism	act or practice of; teaching	terrorism, socialism
-less	without	treeless
-ly	in a certain manner; like	seriously, manly
-ness	state or quality	happiness

Section 3 Summary

Israel's Economy

Israel has a harsh landscape. It is hot and dry. There is a shortage of fresh water. A lot of its land is not good for farming. Still, the people of Israel have created a country with a modern economy and lively culture.

Israelis have made farms in the desert. They use **irrigation** to grow fruits, vegetables, cotton, and other crops. The Sea of Galilee is a freshwater lake in northern Israel. The Israelis pump water from the lake through canals and pipelines. To create more farmland, Israelis drained Lake Hula and nearby swamps in the 1950s.

Another reason for the success of Israeli agriculture is cooperation. Most of Israel's farmers live in small villages called *moshavim*. They share equipment and information about new methods of farming. They also pool their crops so they can get better prices.

About one out of four Israelis works in manufacturing. Most Israeli industry is in high technology. Israel makes high quality electronic and scientific equipment.

Some manufacturing is done in special settlements called kibbutzim. People on a **kibbutz** eat together, work together, and share profits equally. Originally, most kibbutzim centered on farming. But modern farm machinery has reduced the need for farm workers. As a result, many kibbutzim have turned to manufacturing.

The most important part of Israel's economy is the service industry. One type of service industry is trade. Israel is on the Mediterranean Sea. Its main port is Haifa. Many of the products Israel buys and sells pass through Haifa. Israel has few natural resources. It must buy much of what it needs from other countries. ☑

Key Terms

irrigation (ihr uh GAY shun) *n.* the watering of crops using canals and other artificial waterways

kibbutz (kih BOOTS) *n.* a cooperative settlement

Vocabulary Strategy

The suffix *-ing* has several meanings. Some of them are listed in the table on the previous page. Choose the correct meaning to write a definition of *manufacturing*.

____

____

____

✓ Reading Check

What industry is the most important part of the Israeli economy?

____

____

The People of Israel

There are about 6.5 million people in Israel. More than 90 percent of them live in cities.

About 80 percent of the people of Israel are Jews. But there are a lot of differences among them. When Israel was founded in 1948, most Jews who moved there were from Europe and North America. Because these people came from countries that were modern, they helped make Israel a modern, developed country. Later, groups of Jews came from other Middle Eastern countries, from Ethiopia in Africa, and from Russia. ✓

✓ Reading Check

Name two areas from which Jewish people have moved to Israel.

1. ______________________

2. ______________________

About 15 percent of Israel's people practice Islam. Most Muslims in Israel are Palestinian Arabs. Before 1948, the region was known as Palestine. Both Jews and Palestinian Arabs believe Palestine is their homeland. Israel won parts of Egypt, Jordan, and Syria through a chain of wars with its Arab neighbors. Arabs call these the "occupied territories." They include the **West Bank**, the **Gaza Strip**, and the Golan Heights.

Target Reading Skill

Look in the bracketed paragraph to find two causes for the disagreements that divide the Israelis and the Palestinians.

____

____

____

____

[For years, there has been violence between the Palestinians and Israelis. People on both sides have tried to make peace, but the violence goes on. One reason is that many Palestinians who left their homes during the Arab-Israeli wars now want to return. But Israelis are against this. Another reason is that many Israelis want to stay in the homes that they built in the occupied territories. But Palestinians are against this.]

Review Questions

1. How do Israeli farmers grow crops in a desert?

____

____

2. What percentage of Israel's population is Muslim?

____

____

Key Terms

West Bank (west bank) *n.* a disputed region on the western bank of the Jordan River

Gaza Strip (GAHZ uh strip) *n.* a disputed region on the Mediterranean coast

CHAPTER 8

Prepare to Read

Section 4
Saudi Arabia: Oil and Islam

Objectives

1. Learn how oil has affected Saudi Arabia's development and economy.
2. Discover how Islam affects everyday life in Saudi Arabia.
3. Understand the main features of Saudi Arabia's government.

Target Reading Skill

Understand Effects Remember that a cause makes something happen. The effect is what happens as a result of the cause. Just as an effect can have more than one cause, a cause can have more than one effect. You can find the effect or effects by answering the question, "What happened?" If there are several answers to that question, the cause had more than one effect.

As you read this section, find two effects of oil wealth on the development of Saudi Arabia. Then find two effects of Islam being the main religion. Write your findings in a chart like the one below.

What happened because oil was discovered in Saudi Arabia?	What happens in everyday life in Saudi Arabia because of Islam?
• •	• •

Vocabulary Strategy

Finding Roots Syllables or groups of syllables are often added at the beginning or at the end of a word. This creates a new word.

Sometimes the root word changes a little bit before a syllable is added to the end. Often, the final *e* is dropped. For example, we can add the syllable *-y* to the end of the word *ease* to create a new word. It is spelled *easy* (and **not** *easey*!). But you can still recognize the root word. Another example: *dance + ing = dancing* (**not** *danceing*!).

Section 4 Summary

For more than a thousand years, Muslims from all over the world have traveled to the city of Mecca, in Saudi Arabia. Traveling to Mecca is an important part of the Muslim religion. The journey has a name—the **hajj**. Muslims must make the hajj at least once in their lives.

Target Reading Skill

Read the paragraphs under the head "Oil Wealth and Saudi Arabia." Several effects occurred because oil was discovered. List three effects.

1. ______________________

2. ______________________

3. ______________________

Oil Wealth and Saudi Arabia

In 1900, Mecca was a very poor town. Saudi Arabia was one of the poorest countries in the world. Most of Saudi Arabia is covered by desert. Many of its people made a living by herding animals.

In the 1930s, oil was discovered in Southwest Asia. Oil is a valuable natural resource. One of the many products made from oil is gasoline, which is used to run cars. Finding oil changed everything. It made Saudi Arabia rich. Large cities grew and are still growing. When oil prices are high, buildings go up quickly. When oil prices are low, the building comes to a stop. This is because the economy is based on oil.

Saudi Arabia has the biggest oil economy in the world. It has about one fourth of the world's oil. ✓

✓ Reading Check

About how much of the world's oil is in Saudi Arabia?

____

Oil money has changed the lives of all Saudis. Beginning in the late 1960s, the government used money from the sale of oil to modernize the country. It built modern highways, airports, seaports, and a telephone system.

The Saudis also built thousands of schools. The country has eight big universities. In 1900, many Saudis could not read or write. Today, they become doctors, scientists, and teachers.

Everyday Life in Saudi Arabia

In Saudi Arabia, Islam is part of daily life. For example, before a new type of product, such as a cell phone, can be used, the nation's religious leaders study it. They decide whether it goes against Muslim values. If it does, Saudis cannot use it.

Key Term

hajj (haj) *n.* a pilgrimage or journey to Mecca undertaken by Muslims during the month of the hajj

In Saudi Arabia, there are department stores, hotels, and universities. But there are no movie theaters or night clubs. Most Saudis follow a branch of Islam that forbids these kinds of entertainment.

Alcohol and pork are illegal. Shops close five times a day when Muslims pray. Saudis do use some Western inventions. But they make sure that these inventions do not go against Islamic traditions.

Many laws and traditions deal with the role of women. Women are protected in some ways. They are also not allowed to do certain things. For example, Saudi women must cover themselves with a full-length black cloak when they go out in public. That is one rule. Another is that they may not drive cars.

When new schools were built, many women were able to get more education. But boys and girls go to different schools. At the university level, women and men do not study together. Female students take classes from male teachers over a video system.

Most of the rules for daily life come from the **Quran**. The Quran is the holy book of Islam. Muslims view the Quran as a guide for living. ☑

The Government of Saudi Arabia

Islam guides more than daily life in Saudi Arabia. The country's government is based on the Quran. It is an absolute **monarchy** ruled under Islamic law. The king and the royal family make up most of the government. Political parties and elections are not allowed. ☑

Review Questions

1. On what natural resource is Saudi Arabia's economy based?

   ____

   ____

2. How do Muslims view the Quran?

   ____

   ____

Key Terms

Quran (koo RAHN) *n.* the holy book of Islam

monarchy (MAHN ur kee) *n.* a state or a nation in which power is held by a monarch—a king, a queen, or an emperor

Vocabulary Strategy

The words below appear in the paragraphs at left. Their roots were changed slightly when these words were made. Write the root of each word on the line after it. Then circle the words as you read them in your text.

Mark the Text

education ______________

daily ______________

living ______________

✓ Reading Check

Give two examples of how Islam is a part of daily life in Saudi Arabia.

1. ______________

   ____

2. ______________

   ____

✓ Reading Check

What kind of government does Saudi Arabia have?

____

____

CHAPTER 8

Prepare to Read

Section 5
The Stans: A Diverse Region

Objectives

1. Examine the factors that have caused war and conflicts in the Stans.
2. Learn about the economies of the Stans.
3. Discover how environmental issues affect life in the Stans.

Target Reading Skill

Recognize Cause-and-Effect Signal Words As you read, watch for clues that show cause and effect. Often, a word will give you a signal that what is being described is either a cause or an effect. Words such as *affect, as a result*, and *from* signal a cause or effect.

In the following example, *because* signals a cause:

Because the Taliban refused to hand bin Laden over to the United States, American troops invaded Afghanistan in October 2001.

The cause is the Taliban refusing to hand bin Laden to the United States. The effect is American troops invading Afghanistan. As you read, look for words that signal other causes and effects.

Vocabulary Strategy

Using Roots and Suffixes A suffix is one or more syllables attached to the end of a word to make a new word. The word it is attached to is known as the root. When a suffix is added to a root, the new word has a new meaning.

Some common suffixes are listed below, along with their meanings and examples. Notice that some have more than one meaning. Learning to identify suffixes, and knowing what they mean, will help you understand what you read.

Suffix	Meaning	Example
-al	of or like	coastal
-dom	position or domain of; condition of being	kingdom; wisdom
-ic	like or having to do with	angelic
-ist	person who does; believer in	socialist
-ly	in a certain manner; like	seriously; manly

Section 5 Summary

Afghanistan, Kazakhstan, Uzbekistan, Tajikistan, Turkmenistan, and Kyrgyzstan make up the Stans.

Warfare and Unrest in Afghanistan

Afghanistan has been troubled by unrest for many years. The Soviet Union invaded it in 1979. Many people fled to Pakistan. There they lived in **refugee** camps. The Soviet troops withdrew in 1989.

In 1996, a group called the Taliban gained power in Afghanistan. They followed a very strict form of Islam. They made everyone in the country follow their rules. Anyone who violated these rules was killed or harshly punished. Girls were not allowed to attend school.

Osama bin Laden was a Saudi Arabian living in Afghanistan who supported the Taliban. Bin Laden led a terrorist group called al-Qaeda. He was the main suspect in the terrorist attacks of September 11, 2001. Because the Taliban did not hand bin Laden over to the United States, American troops invaded Afghanistan in October 2001. The Americans quickly overthrew the Taliban. ✓

Conflicts in Other Central Asian Countries

Other countries in Central Asia have also had conflicts. Central Asia is a mix of ethnic groups and cultures. For many years, strong Soviet rule kept tensions under control. When Soviet rule ended, conflicts erupted.

Kazakhs and Russians have disagreed in Kazakhstan. Civil war raged in Tajikistan through much of the 1990s. It left the country in ruins. Extreme Muslims in Uzbekistan tried to overthrow the government.

Some governments in the region took away political freedoms and violated human rights. Several countries have turned toward **dictatorship**. Some Western countries have started to help the Stans. They have given money to help the countries build democracies. ✓

Key Terms

refugee (ref yoo JEE) *n.* a person who flees war or other disasters

dictatorship (DIK tay tur ship) *n.* a form of government in which power is held by a leader who has absolute authority

Vocabulary Strategy

The word below appears on this page. It contains a suffix. Underline the suffix. Then write the definition of the suffix on the lines provided.

freedom

____

____

Mark the Text

Add the meaning of the suffix to the meaning of the root word. What does *freedom* mean?

____

____

____

✓ Reading Check

What happened in Afghanistan after the terrorist attacks on September 11, 2001?

____

____

✓ Reading Check

What have some Western countries done to help the countries of Central Asia?

____

____

____

Economic Conditions in Central Asia

The Stans are mainly poor countries. Farming is the backbone of their economies. However, other industries are growing.

During the Soviet era, large cotton farms produced huge amounts of cotton for export. Cotton farming is still important. But more grains, fruits, and vegetables are being grown, and more livestock is being raised. ✓

✓ Reading Check

Other than cotton, what important types of crops are grown in Central Asia?

Central Asian cities are growing. Many people live in apartments and work in offices or factories. Many of the factories are old and don't work well. Some are being updated.

Several of the Stans are rich in oil, natural gas, and other minerals. Foreign companies would like to export these resources. However, one problem is that these countries are **landlocked**. Pipelines are planned to carry oil and gas out of the region.

Environmental Issues

Target Reading Skill

What words in the bracketed paragraph signal a cause of pollution in Central Asia?

[The Soviet Union hurt the environment of Central Asia. For years, it did nuclear tests in northern Kazakhstan. Because of these tests, the region has terrible radiation pollution. Radiation has hurt the people who live nearby. The pollution will take years to clean up.]

Another major problem is the drying of the Aral Sea. For years, the Soviets took water from rivers that feed the sea. As a result, it is now drying up. ✓

✓ Reading Check

How have environmental problems affected the Stans?

However, large parts of Central Asia are still untouched. They are a key resource for the region.

Review Questions

1. What is the main economic activity in the Stans?

2. How has nuclear testing affected Kazakhstan?

Key Term

landlocked (LAND lahkt) *adj.* having no direct access to the sea

Chapter 8 Assessment

1. For many years, India and Pakistan have fought over an area called
   A. Kashmir.
   B. the Stans.
   C. Taliban.
   D. Haifa.

2. Pakistan's economy is based mostly on
   A. farming.
   B. the textile industry.
   C. carpets.
   D. hydroelectricity.

3. The most important part of the Israeli economy is
   A. agriculture.
   B. manufacturing.
   C. service industries.
   D. tourism.

4. Muslims from around the world must travel to Mecca in Saudi Arabia
   A. to buy cheap gasoline.
   B. to get a good education.
   C. to vote in Saudi Arabian elections.
   D. to complete the religious trip known as the hajj.

5. Several countries of Central Asia have turned toward
   A. absolute monarchies.
   B. democracies.
   C. dictatorships.
   D. constitutional monarchies.

Short Answer Question

Why has there been continued conflict between Israelis and Palestinians?

____

____

____

____

CHAPTER 9

Prepare to Read

Section 1
Vietnam: A Nation Rebuilds

Objectives

1. Find out how Vietnam was divided by conflicts and war.
2. Learn how Vietnam has rebuilt its economy.

Target Reading Skill

Identify Main Ideas It is hard to remember every detail that you read. Good readers are able to find the main ideas of the text they are reading. The main idea is the most important point of a section of text. It summarizes all the other points, or details.

To find the main idea of a paragraph, read it through once. Then ask yourself what the paragraph is about. Do all the sentences center on the same point? If so, you've found the main idea. Sometimes, it is stated in the first sentence or two.

The main idea of the paragraph below is underlined:

> <u>In the early 1970s, the fighting spread.</u> North Vietnam was sending supplies to its troops through the nearby nations of Laos and Cambodia. The United States bombed this supply route and then invaded Cambodia. The South Vietnamese attacked Laos.

As you read this section, look for the main idea of each paragraph.

Vocabulary Strategy

Recognizing Signal Words Signal words are words or phrases that prepare you for what is coming next.

There are different kinds of signal words. Often signal words tell you the order in which events happen. These are sequence signal words. Some sequence signal words are shown below. Use these words to help you keep track of events as you read.

first	next	then
finally	before	earlier
later	from May to July	in 1959

Section 1 Summary

Decades of Conflict and War

Vietnam went through a long period of conflict. From 1946 to 1954, the Vietnamese fought together to defeat France. Then Vietnam was divided into two nations. Communists ruled North Vietnam. The United States supported the non-communist government of South Vietnam. Elections were promised to unite Vietnam under one government.

Instead there was a **civil war**. The elections were not held because the United States and the leaders of South Vietnam feared that the Communists might win. This worried the leaders of the United States because they believed in the **domino theory**. This theory said that if the Communists won in Vietnam nearby nations would become Communist, too.

In 1959, the Communists started a war to take over the South. Their leader, Ho Chi Minh (hoh chee min), wanted all of Vietnam to be one Communist nation. At first, the United States sent military advisors to help South Vietnam. Later, hundreds of thousands of American troops arrived to fight the Communist troops, called the Viet Cong. By 1968, there were more than 500,000 American troops in Vietnam. ✓

In the early 1970s, the fighting spread. North Vietnam was sending supplies to its troops through the nearby nations of Laos and Cambodia. The United States bombed this supply route and then invaded Cambodia. The South Vietnamese attacked Laos.

Thousands of American soldiers were being hurt or killed in Vietnam. Many Americans wanted the war to end. In 1973, the United States pulled its troops out of Vietnam. More than 3 million Americans had served in the Vietnam War.

Key Terms

civil war (SIV ul wawr) *n.* a war between political parties or regions within the same country

domino theory (DAHM uh noh THEE uh ree) *n.* a belief that if one country fell to communism, neighboring nations would also fall, like a row of dominoes

Vocabulary Strategy

Mark the Text

Find and circle all the sequence signal words and phrases on this page.

✓ Reading Check

Why did North Vietnam launch a war against South Vietnam?

After the Vietnam War

North Vietnam conquered South Vietnam in 1975. The country was then reunited. It had a Communist government. Vietnam had been badly hurt by the war. More than a million people had been killed or wounded. And Vietnam needed to rebuild homes, farms, and factories destroyed in the war.

However, the Vietnamese economy was not growing. Vietnam had to make some changes. Vietnam is still a Communist country today. But now the government lets some people run their own businesses. That means it uses the free enterprise system. This has improved the lives of many Vietnamese.

Vietnam's biggest success has been in rebuilding its cities. Hanoi, in the north, is the capital. The wealthiest city is Ho Chi Minh City. It used to be called Saigon, when it was the capital of South Vietnam. Today, it is a center of trade. ☑

Some Vietnamese who live in the cities have more money than other Vietnamese. They can afford many of the same things Americans enjoy. Many of them run businesses that help Vietnam's economy.

Vietnam's economy grew quickly during most of the 1990s. People from other countries began to invest their money in Vietnam's businesses. Farming doubled. Vietnam no longer had to buy its food from other countries. Instead, it became one of the countries that sells a very large amount of rice to other nations.

✓ Reading Check

Which city in Vietnam is the wealthiest and also the nation's center of trade?

____

____

Target Reading Skill

Which sentence in the bracketed paragraph states the main idea of the paragraph?

____

____

____

Review Questions

1. Describe the roles that the United States played in the Vietnam War.

____

____

____

2. In what ways has Vietnam had success in rebuilding its economy?

____

____

____

CHAPTER 9

Prepare to Read

Section 2
Australia: A Pacific Rim Country

Objectives

1. Learn about the major economic activities in Australia.
2. Find out how Aboriginal people in Australia are working to improve their lives.

Target Reading Skill

Identify Supporting Details The main idea of a paragraph or section is its most important point. The main idea is supported by details. Details give more information about the main idea. They may explain the main idea. They may give additional facts or examples. They tell you *what, where, why, how much,* and *how many.*

The main idea of the section titled "Aborigines: Improving Lives" is stated in this sentence: "Aboriginal leaders have worked to make the lives of their people better." As you read, notice how the details tell you more about the life of the Aborigines and how things are changing for them.

Vocabulary Strategy

Recognizing Signal Words Signal words are words or phrases that give you clues. They help you understand what you read. They prepare you for what is coming next.

There are different kinds of signal words. Signal words may be used to show relationships, such as contrast. Contrast shows the differences between things or ideas.

Some signal words that show contrast are listed below. Use these words to help you understand what you are reading in this section.

but	however
not	on the other hand
even though	yet
despite	

Section 2 Summary

Economic Activities

Australia used to be a colony of Great Britain. Since Australia became independent, its population has become very diverse. That means that people from many different nations and backgrounds have come to make Australia their home.

Today, Australia has close ties with other nations of the Pacific Rim. The Pacific Rim countries border the Pacific Ocean. They include Japan, South Korea, China, and Taiwan. The United States is another major Pacific Rim nation. It is one of Australia's main trading partners. Australia's economy depends on trade with Pacific Rim countries.

Target Reading Skill

What details in the bracketed paragraph explain the meaning of the "Pacific Rim"?

Australia sends products to many countries in Asia. Large cargo ships carry Australian cattle, wool, and meat to markets in other countries. They also carry Australian minerals to Japan.

Only 7 percent of Australia's land is good for farming. Most of this land is in southeastern Australia and along the east coast. The country's few rivers are in those areas. Farmers use the rivers to irrigate their crops. Australia's most important crop is wheat. Australia is one of the world's leading wheat growers.

Ranching is also important to Australia's economy. Sheep and cattle provide meat for sale to other countries. Australia is the world's leading wool producer. Most cattle and sheep are raised on large ranches called stations. Some of the largest stations are in the **outback**. Few people live in this hot, dry region. ✓

✓ Reading Check

How does ranching help Australia's economy?

In the outback, there is little grass for the animals to eat. That is why stations are so large. There is one outback station that covers nearly 12,000 square miles (31,080 square kilometers)—that is larger than the state of Maryland! In the outback, ranchers use **artesian wells** to supply water for their cattle.

Key Terms

outback (OWT bak) *n.* the dry land consisting of plains and plateaus that makes up much of central and western Australia
artesian well (ahr TEE zhun wel) *n.* a well in which water flows under natural pressure without pumping

Aborigines: Improving Lives

Aboriginal people were the earliest people of Australia. Today, they are working hard to save their culture. They are also taking a bigger part in Australia's economy. For example, Aboriginal people now own their own companies.

Aboriginal leaders have worked to make the lives of their people better. Their schools now teach Aboriginal languages. Aborigines mark important events with songs and dances. These songs and dances have been passed down from parents to children for hundreds of years. Artists are also helping bring attention to Aboriginal culture. They create traditional rock paintings and tree bark paintings.

Aboriginal leaders have helped their people in another important way. They helped the government of Australia understand that it had to make changes. The government has begun to give Aboriginal land back to Aborigines. The government has built schools and hospitals on their land. It has also begun to protect some of the places that are important in Aboriginal religion.

Aborigines have more rights now. But their main goal is to get back the lands that used to belong to their people. The courts have helped them to achieve this goal. However, many ranchers and farmers now live on those lands. They do not want to give the land back. It may take many years to work out the solution to this problem. ☑

Vocabulary Strategy

Mark the Text

In the last paragraph, two signal words are used to show contrast. Find the signal words and circle them.

✓ Reading Check

What is a main goal for Aboriginal people in Australia today?

Review Questions

1. Why do few people make their home in Australia's outback?

2. Give two examples showing how Aboriginal leaders have worked to improve the lives of their people.

Chapter 9 Assessment

1. What did the United States fear might happen if it did not help South Vietnam fight against North Vietnam?
   A. The French would take control.
   B. North Vietnam would attack China.
   C. Communists would take over South Vietnam.
   D. The United States would lose control of North Vietnam.

2. Today, Vietnam is
   A. divided into two nations.
   B. a Communist nation that allows some free enterprise.
   C. one of the richest countries in Asia.
   D. still unable to rebuild its cities.

3. Some of Australia's trading partners in the Pacific Rim include China, Taiwan,
   A. India, and France.
   B. Italy, and the United States.
   C. Britain, and New Zealand.
   D. Japan, and the United States.

4. Where are some of Australia's largest ranches, or stations, located?
   A. in the southeast part of the country
   B. along the east coast
   C. on the west coast
   D. in the outback

5. How are Aborigines working to improve the lives of their people?
   A. Their schools now teach Aboriginal languages.
   B. They play a bigger part in Australia's economy.
   C. Their artists help bring attention to their culture.
   D. all of the above

Short Answer Question

How has Vietnam changed since the end of the Vietnam War?

____

____

____

____